# DOORS OF HOPE

**Advocate. Influence. Protect.**

**by Sylvia Rivera**

*Unless otherwise specified, Scripture quotations are taken from The Holy Bible. The NIV Study Bible. New International Version. Copyright © 1985. International Bible Society. Zondervan Corporation.*

***Doors of Hope: Advocate. Influence. Protect***
© 2018

by Sylvia Rivera

door2close2open@gmail.com

*No part of this book may be reproduced, stored in a retrieval system, or transmitted in any form or by any means— electronically, mechanical, photocopy, recording, or otherwise— without prior written permission of the publisher except in the case of brief quotations used in articles and review.*

ISBN 13: 978-1987733822

To order copies of this book, please go to Amazon and Kindle.

Or go to www.doorsofhope.online

Cover art by Chris Jeanguenat (www.ebsqart.com). Used with permission.

Dedicated to parents, teachers,

leaders, and others

who desire to influence

girls, tweens, and teens

to act more wisely against

the real threat of

being abused, exploited,

and trafficked.

In gratitude

to Jesus,

the only source of genuine hope,

and

to my husband Max,

whose love inspires me.

# Contents

**The Setting**

    1    Advocates Needed    11

    2    The Challenge    15

            Victim Reports 15

            Definitions 21

            Stats We Need to Know 23

            Our Hope 25

            Slavery and Abolition Again? 27

            Minds and Methods of Exploiters/Traffickers 29

    3    All About Girls    33

            Heart's Desires and Culture 33

            Truth Needed 42

**Learn to Influence**

| | | |
|---|---|---|
| 4 | Scientific Influence Models Made Simple | 51 |

        Our Responsibilities 51

        Automatic Reactions 53

        Systematic Process 58

        Heuristic Method 59

        Rhetorical Method 59

        Attribution Theory 60

        Conditioning Theory 60

        Cognitive Dissonance Theory 60

        Functional Theory 61

        Narrative Transportation Theory 62

        Social Judgment Theory 62

        Force 63

        Crucial Conversations 63

        Elaboration Likelihood Model 64

        Online Persuasion 65

|   |   |
|---|---|
|   | Integrated Ethical Framework 66 |
| 5 | Exploring Biblical Models of Influence 67 |
|   | Free Will 68 |
|   | Questions 69 |
|   | Suffering 72 |
|   | Truth in Love 74 |
|   | Modeling 76 |
|   | Storytelling 78 |
|   | Conviction and Power 82 |
|   | Melt 85 |
|   | Process 87 |

**Plan for Action**

|   |   |
|---|---|
| 6 | Best Practices for Influencing Girls 91 |
|   | Pulling It All Together 91 |
|   | Critical Component <u>Before</u> You Start 93 |
|   | Sample Plans 94 |

Your Turn to Create Plans 114

Testimony of a Changed Life 114

| 7 | Invite Others | 117 |

Suggestions 119

**Endnotes**      123

**About the Author**      139

**Other Books by Author**      141

**Resources**      143

# The Setting

# 1

# Advocates Needed

"Urgent!" was the message.

My friend Christine periodically checks her teen daughter's smart phone to nip in the bud any potential harm.[1] After seeing nothing dangerous for months, she was shocked to find nude photos of a man along with conversations with him for the past week or so. She messaged me to pray for wisdom since she and her husband planned a serious conversation with their daughter that evening.

Ellie initially responded angrily, "How dare you look at my phone!"

They discovered that the explicit photos their daughter received were not from someone she knew at school (although that carries its own potential dangers too) but from an adult living who-knows-where, with who-knows-what-history, and with everyone-can-guess-what-motives. Ellie had devoted many hours to him online and thought of him as her boyfriend.

Practically everyone, whether children, tweens, teens, or adults, carries a smart phone as well as has a tablet and/or a laptop. Everyone includes scammers, abusers, exploiters, and traffickers who employ those tools to weave a "friendly" but evil snare. Nita Belles, coordinator for Oregonians Against Trafficking Humans, asserts that "the internet serves as a virtual clearinghouse, a sex bazaar connecting demand and supply."[2]

All girls, tweens, teens, and young women face the danger of being abused, exploited, and trafficked, not just online but in everyday places such as malls and schools. Boys are also at risk of abuse and exploitation, although at a much lower rate. They all need the effective and positive influence of parents, teachers, and leaders for new awareness and understanding so that they are enabled to choose to make changes in their decisions and actions for their own protection. (Although boys need positive influence too, this book's focus is on girls. The methods of influence presented here would be similar for boys but would need a masculine understanding for adaptation. Hopefully another book will be written by a man for boys.)

**By the way, "girls" is the term I will use throughout this book to simplify the wordy phrase "girls, tweens, teens, and young women." Sometimes I may use the term "daughters" when appropriate.**

Most girls are unaware or uninformed of the real, serious, present threat of abuse, exploitation, and trafficking. Most believe that abuse, exploitation, and trafficking could never affect them, only *certain other* girls. Yet their enemies have crafted the ability to appear to be the answer to their universal search for acceptance and love. Perpetrators take advantage of their unawareness, vulnerability, and basic need for love as well as the influence of our hyper-sexualized culture.

Parents and those interested in positively influencing girl's welfare need to know the answer to these questions: What are the facts about this threat? What are the *most effective* means of influencing girls so that they make wiser decisions to avoid abuse, exploitation, and trafficking?

This book compiles and analyzes research to educate parents, leaders, mentors, and teachers, and then presents the most effective means of influencing girls so that they may be protected from the physical, emotional, and spiritual damage of abuse, exploitation, and trafficking. You'll read:

- ✓ Real life reports of victimized girls
- ✓ Definitions of abuse, exploitation, and trafficking

- ✓ Data about the prevalence of sexual exploitation
- ✓ Methods of abusers, exploiters, and traffickers
- ✓ Vulnerabilities of girls
- ✓ Contemporary cultural influences that expose girls to harm
- ✓ Biblical and scientific models of influence
- ✓ Specific suggestions for applying the best influencing methods

The goal of this book is that you will be well equipped to have a positive influence on girls' lives so that they act wisely to better protect themselves. My vision is that readers will put into practice what they learn here and then will celebrate with empowered girls who have learned to stand against the possibilities of harm. Also, I envision that abusers, exploiters, and traffickers will be increasingly unsuccessful at seducing and trapping their intended victims.

Join me on this journey of facing the challenge and discovering the best practices for influencing girls to be prudent about self-protection.

# 2

# The Challenge

**Victims' Reports**

Theresa Flores was new in town because her father's good-paying executive position required that the family move often.[3] She was lonely, trying to make friends at high school. She met a guy at school and hung out with him and his friends at school and at church for about six months.

One day, he offered to give Theresa a ride home after school. She felt relief, not having to walk home alone, but Theresa felt uneasy when he headed away from her house. He explained that he needed to get something at his house first. When the car stopped in front of his house, she stayed in her seat to wait for him to return. He invited her to come in, but she said no.

He then stuck his head in through her open window, gave her an irresistible smile, and said the magic words all girls want to hear, "You know, I really love you." Touched by that, although a little nervous about going inside, she walked up to the house with him.

No one else seemed to be at home. He offered her a seat and brought her a glass of soda to sip while he went to retrieve what he needed. The next thing she remembers is waking up in the bedroom having been sexually assaulted. Shame consumed her. Things only got worse.

A few days later, her "boyfriend" showed her the photos that had been taken of her at his house. That afternoon she answered the home phone to hear an older, gruff male voice warning her that the photos would be shown to her parents and that her brothers would be killed if she did not cooperate with him. He hissed, "Be in front of your house at midnight, or else." By the way, this type of boyfriend is called a "Romeo pimp," and his job is to bring girls to the trafficker for financial gain and control.

That was the first night of her living hell, sneaking out of her beautiful home in the suburbs in the dark to be taken places where she was beaten and sexually exploited, with multiple men in nightmarish ways. One night, one of the men asked her so-called boyfriend, "What's her name?" He said, "It doesn't matter." Theresa was dehumanized, a nameless object for profit.

After two years she escaped, thanks to another job transfer for her father to a new location. Theresa left town without telling anyone where she was going. Those phone calls were to a phone number that was no longer in service.

It is rare for girls to escape once they have been snared because of the evil threats and physical abuse with which they are pommeled into absolute compliance. For *potential* victims, it is a blessing that those few who do find freedom want to share their stories. These courageous girls want to prevent others from going through the horribly painful nightmare.

Theresa Flores wrote a book called *Slave Across the Street: Blackmailed into Sex Trafficking*.[4] Also, she travels around the United States to warn young women of the danger that lurks in ordinary American communities. She declares that she recovered from her living nightmare through years of counseling together with Jesus' love and healing power.

Most people think of the girls who are abused, exploited, and trafficked as coming from foreign countries or from the rough, impoverished, urban areas in the United States. Many victims do fit those stereotypes, but the truth is closer to you and your family than you imagine. The threat is in your own neighborhood wherever you live.

Theresa's story is not uncommon: a two-parent family, Christians, good income, beautiful home, educated; the girl has a nice new boyfriend, dreams of romance and love, fears losing him, trusts him completely after knowing him for a while; and then she makes decisions that break some of her parents' rules—such as getting a ride or entering a house without their knowledge or permission—all because she is "in love."

Nita Belles, who labors to raise awareness of the dangers of sex trafficking, says: "One of the biggest obstacles to stopping human trafficking in the United States is that people don't believe it can happen to them or to their loved ones. Anyone regardless of her economic and social status, can fall into the hands of traffickers and pimps. We are living in a world of false security. Even those teenagers who grow up in solid Christian homes go through times of insecurity, times when they want to experience new things and push against the boundaries and limitations their parents place on them."[5]

Gretchen Smeltzer, founder and executive director of a program called "Into the Light" that brings awareness to teens for prevention of exploitation, agrees. She reports that *all* of Generation Z are at risk and need to know that they are likely to be manipulated and exploited.

Smeltzer shares the story of a girl named Katelyn who was usually wise about keeping herself safe.[6] One day she and her mother had a fight, so she stormed to one of her social websites and posted her raw feelings. One of her longtime "friends" on that site responded by saying she would like to take her out to cheer her up. Yet she was not cheered up but seized for trafficking.

Thankfully, her online post was read by the police after her parents reported her missing. The officers had the information needed to rescue her and to arrest the perpetrator. She was traumatized but quickly returned home to begin the healing process. It could easily have ended more tragically.[7]

It is not always a boyfriend who is the lure. Sometimes it's a *girlfriend* who is used as the decoy on behalf of traffickers. Sarah drove to high school in a new Honda Accord, which her parents had given for her 16th birthday.[8] They had also thrown a party for her with their church's youth group.

The car came with a curfew and the insistence of her parents that they always know where she was and who she was with; they also expected her to find a job to pay the car expenses.

That school-day morning, things hadn't started off well. Her mom had told her she must return a shirt that she had bought because it was "too tight and too low." As she drove into the school parking lot, she saw her new friend Maggie wearing the exact shirt that she had been told to return.

Sarah related her mom's demands. Maggie replied, "I'll give you mine tomorrow. Then you just keep it in your locker to wear at school." Maggie added that Sarah's parents were too strict and bragged about her own easygoing parents. The next day, Maggie brought the shirt and another "sexy" one. "Doesn't it feel good to wear what you want to wear? You look so pretty! You're doing the right thing by following your heart," Maggie said.

Sarah later confided in Maggie that she had not been successful in finding a job to pay for the car's expenses. "I can totally set you up," Maggie offered. "All you have to do is go out with this old guy. You'll have to kiss a little, but it won't be a big deal. I can get you money." So, Sarah agreed then arrived home from the date before her curfew.

Weeks later, Maggie introduced Sarah to a handsome guy named Alex, with whom she fell in love. Her secret boyfriend bought gifts of clothes, perfume, music, and DVDs. Soon, they had intercourse. Sarah was convinced that he was right for her and believed her parents did not really understand or love her as he did.

Sarah eventually learned that Alex ran the dating service where Maggie worked and through which Maggie had set up dates for Sarah to earn car money.

One day, Alex asked Sarah to move with him to Las Vegas to start their romantic dream life together, explaining that business would be good there. They made plans and met in the school parking lot, where she left her car. Off they sped.

After arriving in Las Vegas, Sarah suffered severe physical abuse and sexual exploitation at the hands of her "boyfriend." That was three months after meeting Maggie who was one of Alex's commercial sex slaves. Maggie's role in trafficking is called a "bottom"; he had demanded that Maggie lure other young women into his "business."

Nearly a year later, the thin and pale Sarah escaped her enslavement when the police made a raid where she had been forced to "work." She was relieved to be reunited with her parents and began the long road to recovery. Rarely do trafficking victims escape or survive their enslavement. Thankfully, Theresa, Katelyn, and Sarah are exceptions to that fact.

The subject of sexual abuse, exploitation, and trafficking has been in the headlines as this book was being written, such as the reports on Olympic girls-gymnastics' doctor Larry Nassar, American film producer Harvey Weinstein, entertainer Bill Cosby, and the explosive #MeToo movement. Also, "Smallville" television star Allison Mack was arrested and charged with sex trafficking in connection with the purported self-help organization called NXIVM. This subject needs to be addressed for the sake of our girls.

## Definitions

Before proceeding, let's more fully understand the terms *abuse*, *exploitation*, and *human trafficking*.

- abuse: misuse; treatment of a person with cruelty or violence, especially regularly or repeatedly; mistreatment; molestation; assault; injury; harm; damage

- exploitation: taking advantage of weak and vulnerable groups within society, especially for financial gain, using violence and lies
- human trafficking: a term for modern slavery; a technical term defined by the U. S. Trafficking Victims Protection Act as "the recruitment, harboring, transporting, obtaining, or maintaining of a person *by means of force, fraud, or coercion* for purposes of *involuntary* servitude, debt bondage, slavery, or any commercial sex acts in which the person performing the act is under 18 years old." In summary, it is being treated as someone else's property, not as a human being.[9]

All three of these terms mean dehumanization and objectification.

*Other important definitions* are:

- injustice: the abuse of power that oppresses the vulnerable through violence and lies[10]
- justice: bringing right order and exerting life-giving power to protect the vulnerable[11]

"All abuse and exploitation of human beings is an offense against humankind and God. Slavery robs individuals of their God-given liberty and dignity and is an insult to God who created everyone in His image and for His purpose. Instead of closeness, mutual fulfillment, and a deep exchange of affection, sex becomes solely about the buyer's desires," explains Beth Grant and her collaborators who work against trafficking.[12]

Sex is an integral part of the self. When it is treated as a something to be taken, the person is robbed of human dignity.

**Stats We Need to Know**

No community is immune from the activity of human trafficking. A book titled *In Our Backyard* communicates its proximity. The statistics listed below are estimates based on the research of officials and experts.

Please read these statistics carefully to allow for full impact and understanding.

- ✓ *Online predators'* presence has drastically increased because of the expanding access of children under 18 years of age to the internet and various social networking sites.[13]
- ✓ *Internet access* by 5- to 7-year-olds is about 82 percent; by 8- to 11-year-olds it is about 96 percent; by 12- to 15-year-olds it is about 99 percent.[14]
- ✓ About 75 percent of all *internet-initiated sex crimes* are against girls, with a large majority of them being between 13 and 15 years of age.[15]
- ✓ An estimated 90 percent of children ages 8 to 16 have seen *online pornography*; some of those are through

some gaming sites where graphic nude photos are posted.[16]
- ✓ The U. S. National Center for Missing and Exploited Children *estimates* that of the more than 25,000 reported as *runaway children* under age 18 in 2017 about one in seven of them is likely a victim of sex trafficking.[17]
- ✓ About one-third of *teen runaways* will be trapped into sex slavery within 48 hours of leaving home.[18]
- ✓ The Federal Bureau of Investigation has reported the one-year count of *missing children and teens* was 466,949; of those, 54 percent were girls; 57 percent were white and/or Hispanic; 39 percent were African American.[19]
- ✓ Most children and teens report having experienced some form of *physical assault*, including sexual victimization.[20]
- ✓ In about eight of ten cases of *rape*, the victim knew the person who assaulted them; one in five women are sexually assaulted while in college; about 63 percent of university men have self-reported as having raped or attempted to rape women; about 63 percent of rapes are not reported to the police.[21]
- ✓ The U. S. Department of Justice has *prosecuted trafficking cases* in every state.[22]
- ✓ Estimated *revenue* for traffickers internationally is reported to be about $150 billion per year, second only to drug trafficking.[23]

✓ *Worldwide*, about 46 million people are being trafficked, with most of them being trafficked for commercial sexual exploitation and the rest being used for slave labor.[24]

**Our Hope**

Yet we have hope. Many people are actively working to make the risks known, to educate girls for prevention, to improve laws, to rescue victims, and to restore survivors. We who work in anti-trafficking believe that God created each of us in His image and He desires that each person live with dignity. It is a gross indignity when people are treated as commodities and brutalized. God weeps over those who are exploited.

My heart has been broken by what breaks His. My body shook with sobs when I came to the realization that sexual exploitation and slavery dehumanizes girls *everywhere* nowadays. We modern-day abolitionists work to end slavery. We offer God's hope, healing, and restoration through Jesus Christ to the dehumanized as well as His wisdom for the prevention of exploitation.

David Batstone, professor of ethics at the University of San Francisco and founder of the organization "Not for Sale," writes: "Powerful forces aim to turn human beings into commodities that can be bought and sold like any other piece of property. To declare 'not for sale' affirms that every individual has the inalienable right to be free, to pursue a God-given destiny. We live right now at one of those epic moments in the fight for human freedom."[25]

Additionally, God's heart breaks for the corrupt abusers and traffickers who not only must face the legal consequences of their crimes but also need to repent of their sins. They need a different kind of freedom. Jesus Christ died on the cross to pay the penalty for *all* sin, even for the most heinous of sins. He longs that *all* would come to Him humbly in repentance to put their faith in Him.

The Lord graciously extends the gift of freedom from sin and from its eternal penalty when a person calls out to Jesus and commits to follow Him. As God opens doors, we *can* minister to and pray for slave masters, buyers, and users in the hope that they will turn to Him.

We *can* partner with God to make a difference in this complex and seemingly impossible challenge. We *can* pray and offer ourselves to serve in many ways, which will be explained later. Once we recognize that what is happening in the world endangers girls, we dare not turn our backs. We need to take a stand, speak up, and do whatever we can to protect them and to end the threat.

Batstone encourages us to "not underestimate your own potential and abandon hope for those trapped in captivity."[26] As Edmund Burke, a philosopher and Irish politician of the 19th century, ironically stated, "All that is necessary for the triumph of evil is that good men [and women] do nothing."[27]

It is crucial that we face the truth of exploitation and not diminish, dismiss, or deny it just because we feel uncomfortable, awkward, and fearful. Those are our natural tendencies and feelings. It is my hope that you will take courage, be inspired, and become prepared to be part of the solution. Every person, all of us together, can make a difference.

**Slavery and Abolition Again?**

Although slavery was abolished in England in 1833 and in the United States in 1865, it has never completely vanished. In fact, we are now faced with a great resurgence that has expanded slavery to be more massive than ever before.

"In our own day, a thriving black market in human beings has emerged once again. *More* slaves are in bondage today than were bartered in four centuries of the transatlantic slave trade. Slavery likely crosses our path on a regular basis without our awareness. Seemingly 'upstanding' citizens can be involved," reports Batstone. "There is not a country in the world where slavery could be considered legal. Yet slavery still thrives," says Batstone.[28]

Becoming aware of the growing horrors of injustice and slavery worldwide in 1997, attorney Gary Haugen established a human rights agency called International Justice Mission (IJM) to rescue thousands, to protect millions, to prove that justice for the poor is possible, and to seek the conviction of the criminals involved. IJM supports corps of local advocates who provide direct service to the poor and to victims of violent abuse and oppression. The agency also supports teams of lawyers, investigators, social workers, and community activists.

They advocate that the best solution is home-grown, highly-contextualized remedies together with the best of whatever is needed from external sources. The key to setting people free is radical criminal justice reform, using collaborative casework.[29]

The Trafficking Victims Protection Act (TVPA) was passed by the United States Congress in October of 2000. The TVPA provided legal rights for enslaved victims and access to services instead of being wrongly treated as criminals, as formerly had occurred.

The law also directed the State Department to produce an annual report that evaluates the performance of the governments of every nation worldwide, based on certain standards that the law established, to be a tangible incentive for action by those governments if they aspire to avoid stiff sanctions by the United States.[30]

Katherine Chon and Derek Ellerman, as Brown University students in 2001, started the Polaris Project to shine a spotlight on modern-day slavery. "Once a trafficking ring is exposed to the public eye, the slave holders become more vulnerable to arrest, and slaves are more likely to be rescued," reports Batstone.³¹ Through the years, the Project has promoted the establishment of human trafficking research centers at other colleges and universities. As significant information is garnered, the Project hands over what they have uncovered to service agencies, government agencies, and the media for follow up.

In September of 2003, U. S. President George W. Bush addressed the United Nations about human trafficking, explaining that women and children are the targets of slavery worldwide fueled by organized crime. Bush also created an ambassador position in the U. S. State Department to be a motivator in other countries to make changes to combat modern slavery.³²

## Minds and Methods of Exploiters/Traffickers

As we learned through the TVPA's definition, trafficking victims are *forced, deceived,* and *coerced* into a situation that was unknown and unchosen by them. This was observed in the reports you read earlier.

To explain the ensnaring process, Belles says:

> First, the perpetrator begins wooing the victim [also known as "grooming" the victim]—and there's no one more charming than a person who plans to ultimately

try to control his or her victim through physical and emotional abuse.

 Even those perpetrators who aren't particularly charming don't initiate the discussion by overtly saying, "Hey, I'm going to beat the ___ out of you if you don't do what I want." [The perpetrator] comes to you and says, in various words, "You are the most beautiful girl I have ever see. We could build a beautiful life together."

They initially use flattery, gifts, and promises to build on the romantic hopes of the girls.[33]

Michael Garcia, an attorney and Associate Judge in the New York Court of Appeals, says that they "profit by turning dreams into nightmares."[34]

Who do the predators look for? A 10- to 15-year-old brings in more money for their "business" than do older girls, so they are prime targets in shopping malls, in and near schools, on social internet sites, and anywhere else girls spend their time. Besides flattery and romantic relationships, pimps also post ads for modeling, singing, acting, and dancing jobs to lure in their prey.

To understand the mind of predators, here is a summary of an interview conducted in Dallas, Texas with an incarcerated pimp, "With arrogance, this man described how he and other pimps could walk into any mall in America, and within minutes, walk out with a younger teenage girl who would disappear with him into the world of prostitution."[35] He bragged about having radar for young girls who have low self-esteem and are alone or with a friend.

He would begin a conversation, for example: "Hey, are you OK? You look like something's bothering you. Your family? They don't understand you, do they? Girl, you're beautiful. They don't understand you! You come with me, and I'll give you everything you want." It *can take a little longer* than one conversation at the mall, but they willingly invest time with a girl, telling her everything she is dying to hear while buying her clothes and other valuable items at the mall, until she trusts him enough to walk out to his car.

Once snared by the sticky web of deception, the exploiters' objectives are to eradicate the victim's identity, any sense of personal self-worth, and any sense of rights or boundaries. Tragically, the "boyfriend" and those who work with him employ rape, beatings, starvation, graphic photos of her for blackmail, isolation, drugs, verbal abuse, threats to harm or kill her family members, and many other sordid means of coercion.[36]

People who exploit and enslave girls are so hardened that the concept of human dignity, which means righteousness and justice, is totally absent. They batter the image of God placed in each girl, attempting to destroy her identity, relationships, purpose, talents, and gifts.

Thankfully, no one can destroy the Creator's image imprinted in each of us. But it can be brutalized so that recovery is long and arduous, yet it is possible with God's help.[37] Let's prevent this violent assault on girls, whether by traffickers or other exploiters they meet.

# 3
# All About Girls

### Heart's Desires and Culture

We all want to belong and be valued. Most of us have deep longings for emotional attachment through close relationships. Most girls hope to satisfy their deepest yearnings and to feel complete through one intimate and permanent relationship. Many of them dream of "a home with a spouse to love them and children to nurture."[38]

Girls, ages 10 to 25, have a heightened longing to be accepted and loved, especially by guys. One survey reports *most* but not all, about 90 percent, dream of a lifelong and loving commitment in marriage.[39]

Various cultural influences put girls in jeopardy of not realizing that dream and of being harmed. Educator Eric

Buehrer warns parents about the concept of moral relativity that began being taught in public schools in 1990. He relates that a student who had just completed his ninth-grade health class told his parents, "My values may not be your values, and we certainly can't push our morality on any of my friends; everyone takes his own path to right and wrong." This was a radical shift from his formerly strong Christian values.[40] That concept has become a cultural norm and is affecting students' dreams and their ideas of how to achieve them.

Moral relativity was started to encourage cultural sensitivity. Educators began to teach that philosophy in the name of globalization with its assumed requisite to promote harmony and cooperation. They asserted that absolutes unnecessarily lock us into conflicts and that, therefore, acceptance of ambiguity is to be valued. They labeled absolutes as myths and pushed for tolerance. This philosophy, with its situational ethics, has affected law, justice, morality, and integrity. If social and moral judgments are nothing more than preferences, then those with the loudest voices have the greatest influence.

The voices teens hear are blaring through movies, television, ads, and online social media, which promote sexuality without commitment and sexuality as the means to achieve commitment. When relativity is assumed true, then people who raise a voice in favor of abstinence, purity, and marriage, and against sexual abuse, exploitation, and slavery are labeled as ethnocentric, intolerant, or fanatical. Believers in the Bible and God's perfectly wise law are ridiculed.

The irony is that cultural relativism is like a religion; its dogma defines ultimate reality as all cultures being equally right, and no one can be wrong. Their premise is illogical and unproven yet asserted adamantly, even though, conflicting cultural and religious beliefs obviously cannot be equally right.[41] I affirm that one true living and loving God exists whose perfectly wise biblical parameters are for our good and for the welfare of girls seeking love.

Another cultural concern is that most girls may not see a healthy marriage at home or in the media. Many girls have little idea of what a relatively healthy family looks like (of course, none is perfect). But with the breakdown of the nuclear family and the rise in the number of single mothers in the past 50 years, daughters' vulnerability to sexual abuse and exploitation increases. This also results in many feeling an intense loneliness.[42]

"Without fathers, and in a school-system that long ago gave up any attempt to impart enduring values, these young people are left to sort out their fates according to their own 'lights'," says Bennett. "The media they absorb cannot help them."[43] Risks for those girls raised in fatherless homes include suicide, running away, behavior disorders, dropping out of high school, drug abuse as well as vulnerability to predators.[44]

Also, today's highly sensuous culture is influencing girls. One survey reports that about 75 percent of children say they learned about sex from television and movies.[45] Sexuality increasingly dominates movie screens as well as advertisements, television shows, clothing, and music.

Even some names of makeup and nail polish for girls include names such as Hot Pants, Dirty, Hard Candy, Pimp, and Porn, which distorts girls' minds about sex, while those businesses rake in money. Girls have become accustomed to this casual use of such words as well as seeing sexually provocative images.[46] Thereby, life is more dangerous for our daughters than ever before.[47]

Women are treated by the media more often as objects than as having deep, full value as complete persons. A connection exists between the problem of sexual exploitation and the stories portrayed on screens. Nearly everything girls see tells them that sex is the acme of human experience to be sought after without restraint.[48] Girls have become sexualized and objectified, creating an atmosphere in which sexual predators thrive.[49] "People are not inferior objects to be used and abused for selfish, sexual, sensual pleasure," declares Pastor David Platt.[50]

R. York Moore, author of *Making All Things New,* expresses his concern for the girls who unknowingly find themselves enslaved in commercial sexual exploitation:

> In our day, evil has been romanticized, relegated to the status of myth and portrayed for us as hard-bodied, happy, teenaged vampires. But the myth is all too real as modern-day vampires prey on the flesh of young girls and boys, drinking their youth and absorbing their souls in the brothels where countless children are lost.[51]

Bennett adds: "Our teenage daughters are living in the midst of an epidemic which threatens their physical, sexual, emotional, and mental health every day. Our daughters learn through the constant stream of these messages that their identities and values stem from being sexy. We convince ourselves that sexually charged messages aren't going to change our daughters' behaviors. How wrong we are. [Studies show] that there are both high rates of sexual and physical assaults [and] unacceptably high rates of low self-esteem."[52]

Instant attraction is often portrayed as feeling so good and right. The myth of connecting with the right person through sexual attraction and experience is assumed to be true. Girls are led to believe that everything between a man and a woman can be reduced to sex. So, most girls tend to focus on developing their sexual identity, and they deny their deepest needs and desires. The reality is that people are sexually compatible with far more people than they are relationally. Sexual compatibility should not be the test of relational compatibility. Besides, a couple cannot recognize their relational challenges as quickly and easily when they are physically involved because their glowing sexual feelings blind them. This inhibits and distracts from relationship development necessary for a long-lasting commitment. Sex often masks relational issues, which will surface and cause division *after* the intangible glow wears off. *A couple will be sexually compatible with the right person not vice versa.* Sex is easy. Relationships are not.[53]

It does not help our girls that abstinence has been made to appear "prudish, outdated, and fanatical," which is linked to the fact that all government funding for community-based abstinence education programs and for all risk-avoidance programs have been cut off since 2008.[54]

The antithesis to abstinence is driven by two popular mottos: FOMO, which means "fear of missing out" and YOLO, which means "you only live once."

So, girls, in the hope that their relational needs will be met, give themselves to men. They have been convinced that if they give away their purity, they will be rewarded the prize of a good relationship. Instead, most girls experience a series of intimate boyfriends who refuse to commit to them and then abandon them. Over time, this results in seriously damaged emotions and broken dreams. Their anguish includes trauma, shame, confusion, guilt, fear, regret, and then keeping all these emotions hidden inside.

Increasing that suffering are sexting photos posted online, dating violence, rape, trafficking, sexually transmitted diseases, and unwanted pregnancy followed by an abortion.[55] Bennett reveals that death is a real risk with the college campus hook-up culture and drunken sexual orgies.[56]

Instead of experiencing those devastating effects, Pastor Andy Stanley invites us to "imagine a generation of children who grow up attuned not only to what's happening around them but inside of them as well." Unresolved anger, guilt, greed, and jealousy reduce our resolve against sexual temptation. They tilt us off balance emotionally, leaving us vulnerable to lust." He advises that we teach our children to confess, forgive, give generously, and celebrate the successes of others. These healthy habits keep a heart free from painful clutter and will enable them to more easily resist sexual temptation and to develop a healthy adult relationship. He advises, "These are habits that change everything. Ask your child about what's going on in their hearts."[57]

Another cultural influence that has markedly changed girls' views of sexuality is the commonly held belief that pornography is "a normal part of life, without shame or guilt."[58] It has been reported that about 90 percent of all children, boys and girls, ages 8 through 16 have viewed pornography on the internet, usually using their smart phones or tablets. (By the way, pornography comprises about 12 percent of the internet content).

In addition, one out of 12 children and youth have exchanged messages with sexual content; one out of 25 have sent graphic photos of themselves; and one out of 20 admit to secretly meeting with someone they first met online.

Adolescent minds are still developing, so risk-taking tends to be high while their impulse control is low.[59]

One result for girls is that their capacity to understand and to respect the limits of reality and morality are eroded. It also diminishes their ability to have a meaningful and satisfying sexual relationships later because it affects the neuroplasticity of their brains, which means the reduction of the ability to form new neural connections in response to change.[60] Unfortunately, their impairment is the result of something that is thought to be normal and safe by this generation.[61]

Words have power too. Traditionally, the word "pimp" has been used as a name for a sex trafficker or a commercial sex slave master. Now it has been morphed and adopted into mainstream culture. "Pimped out" means well-dressed; "pimp my hair" means make me look sexy.[62] Even more, the *concept* of a pimp, not just the word, has been mainstreamed as acceptable and sexy through music stars and their lyrics.

"The tipping point came in 2003, when hip-hop star 50 Cents [a.k.a. "Fiddy"] released his platinum-selling song "P.I.M.P.," in which he describes one of the girls working for him as having 'stitches in her head'. Several months later, Reebok rewarded him with a fifty-million-dollar sneaker-deal endorsement," explains Rachel Lloyd, a survivor of commercial sex slavery, an author, and the founder of GEMS to help victims become survivors too.[63]

She identifies other performers who have had big hits and have received awards for their "blatant degradation of women and girls": Hip-hop Snoop Dogg "brought two women on dog leashes to the 2003 MTV Video Music Awards" and has been called by Rolling Stone "America's Most Lovable Pimp"; hip-hop Ice-T is a "self-described former pimp"; rapper Nelly sells "his energy drink called Pimp Juice"; and hip-hop group Three 6 Mafia's song "It's Hard Out Here for a Pimp" was named the Best Original Song for a film during the 78th Academy Awards.[64]

From Lloyd's personal experience with pimps, she sets the record straight, "Pimps are not managers, protectors, or 'market facilitators,' as one research study euphemistically called them, but leeches sucking the souls from beautiful, bright young girls, predators who scour the streets, the group homes, and junior high schools stalking their prey."[65] That's heavy.

Girls are constantly being bombarded by all these lies. We need to raise their awareness of these issues. Prevention of the exploitation of girls is a complex issue because of the multiple root causes reviewed.

Additional vulnerability comes from living with poverty, abuse, instability, as well as the lack of awareness and lack of sufficient support for prevention efforts.[66] Prevention is the only cure that evades the greater challenges of rescue and rehabilitation of victims.[67] So what can we do for the girls in our lives?

**Truth Needed**

We *can* influence girls to learn: to recognize abusive relationships, to end any they are stuck in, and to desire healthy relationships with others.[68] All girls need to be equipped to identify and avoid allowing abusive and unhealthy people to enter their lives. The truth is that great relationships are built on godly decisions, not on strong and sexual emotions. We can wisely direct girls to God and help them discover what is good and best.[69] God has given relational guidelines for our benefit.

The best description of love, the kind that lasts a lifetime, is found in First Corinthians, chapter 13, verses four through seven.

> Love is patient, love is kind. It does not envy, it does not boast, it is not proud. It does not dishonor others, it is not self-seeking, it is not easily angered, it keeps no record of wrongs. Love does not delight in evil but rejoices with the truth. It always protects, always trusts, always hopes, always perseveres.

Sexuality is only "one component of a multifaceted biological, physiological, and psychological miracle that is you," says Stanley.[70] We all desire and need to know another person well, to be known deeply by that person, and to experience full oneness, which is found only in the long-term commitment of marriage. "Sexual purity now, paves the way to intimacy later," he adds. "If relational oneness is something you hope to experience, then save sex for the person with whom you want to become one."[71]

Yet, even still, that relationship will be lacking a firm and lasting foundation if developed without God. "The feeling of significance is crucial to a [person]'s emotional, spiritual, and social stability and is the driving element within the human spirit. This hunger for self-worth is God-given and can *only* be satisfied by Him," writes Robert McGee, a professional counselor.[72] We often fail to turn to God to rely on His steady, uplifting reassurance of who we are. We tend to depend on others for our sense of worth by trying to meet their standards.

The truth is that our true value is based not on our behavior or the approval of others but on what God says is true of us. When we base our worth on the approval of others, then our lives reflect insecurity, fear, and anger. Accepting God's embrace leads to hope, joy, and purpose in life. The answer is to know Jesus, believe in Him, and accept His gift of abundant life. Then the renewal process of the heart and mind of each believer begins by the power of the Holy Spirit so that we focus on the truth of God's unconditional love for us.

A negative thought about ourselves is based on a lie, so we learn how to confront it and overcome it with the truth of God's Word. God wants us to find increasing freedom from enslaving lies as we grow deeper in our relationship with Him. We will still face struggles, but God never gives up on us and our relationships.[73]

"It is the portrait of Christ in the gospel that compels us," Platt says. "We cannot be silent, and we must not be still."[74] He asserts that girls need a Savior who will restore their honor on this earth and renew their hope for all eternity. They do not need condemnation. Fighting exploitation begins with believing, applying, and proclaiming the gospel. The ultimate hope is found in Jesus Christ.[75]

Christian parents, mentors, and the church have a responsibility not only to disciple children and youth to embrace and grow in a personal relationship with Jesus but also to teach them to face the challenges and dangers in the world, using a solid biblical foundation.[76] "We need to start talking to a generation about sexuality instead of dancing around the issue and pretending nobody in church has been affected by it [abuse and exploitation]," says Jim Anderson. He adds that it is "not only affecting those outside the church; it is significantly affecting those inside as well."[77]

We cannot let our discomfort with sexual conversations or our skepticism about the vulnerability of our own girls to abuse and exploitation prevent us from initiating this topic. As seen in the tragic experiences of Theresa and Sarah, narrated in chapter 2, each was the daughter of a Christian family yet was exploited because of their lack of awareness and solid information.

Grant also speaks to believers:

[Our culture] increasingly sells inappropriate sexuality in all its forms as normative [and] our children by default internalize this . . . *unless* Christians parents, leaders, and the church provide them with a healthy, positive, biblical view of sexuality. When our children from elementary school on up are inundated with non-Christian views presented as 'facts,' we as followers of Jesus and the church can no longer afford to remain silent about sexuality. Personal and church discipleship for our children in age-appropriate ways will strengthen them against exploitation while helping them live healthier whole lives as God intended.[78]

She explains: "Many people of faith view sex through the eyes of their secular culture instead of through God's eyes. God's perspective on sex is not an unrestricted secular worldview. Nor is it the prudish view sometimes held by the church. God created sex and presents it as positive and celebratory but with specific boundaries for its protection and enjoyment."[79]

"The truth is that parents or parent surrogates hold all of the power in our daughters' lives," says Bennett. "The time for us to teach our daughters that they do have a choice over whether to be sexually active . . . is far overdue. They feel they have no choice. Our daughters face dangers which threaten to crush their very souls and we cannot stand on the sidelines and shake our heads in wonder any longer."[80]

It is counterculture to say all this, but the truth is that there is only one standard of what is right and good. It is a battle between truth and lies. When we ask questions about what makes a healthy relationship, God's Word is The Source. We can't rely on our own wisdom. We give into temptation too easily. We can't rely on others to inform us with their own wisdom. None of us has perfect wisdom.

We need to encourage girls to put their trust in Jesus and follow the Bible's perfect guidance for wise, good, and healthy decisions. We, as leaders, need to add thorough explanations and allow ample time to answer their questions. Many churches have developed curriculum and booklets on relationships, dating, and marriage to help.[81]

Recommended books on healthy and wise dating are available from several Christian authors. Joshua Harris' book advocates understanding healthy marriage; seeking unromantic/unsexual male and female friends who meet in groups, not as couples; guarding the heart against temptation; setting life goals; knowing the character qualities to look for in friends (among whom one might become your spouse someday in the future); understanding genuine love; and receiving forgiveness from Jesus for your sexual past/maintaining purity.[82]

Authors Dr. Henry Cloud and Dr. John Townsend wrote a book about setting boundaries before beginning to date, which include: what issues do I need to deal with to heal and grow; how to avoid danger; moving too fast; disrespect; and how to grow beyond my desire to look for someone who will cure my loneliness.[83]

I also recommend Andy Stanley's excellent book *The New Rules for Love, Sex & Dating.* He debunks the myth of finding the right person through sexual experience, and he encourages young people, before dating, to focus on becoming a person who would make a good spouse.[84] Other excellent books can be found in Resources at the end of this book.

Now you have a choice: Will you move forward to learn how to effectively influence girls to protect themselves from the predators who attractively lurk at bus stops, schools, malls, on the internet... anywhere young girls go? Or will you continue to ignore the real danger and assume that the girls you are in contact with will never face these threats?

That choice challenged me several years ago when I learned about the rampant exploitation of girls. Now that you know, what will you do? The Lord confronted, convicted, and convinced me to do something about exploitation and modern-day slavery.

Two quotations from eighteenth century abolitionists also motivate me: "You may choose to look the other way, but you can never say that you did not know," said Englishman William Wilberforce.[85] "To be silent... would be criminal," wrote the American Anthony Benezet.[86]

"Refuse to do nothing."[87] Pray and then invest yourself, as they did two-plus centuries ago, by opposing twenty-first century exploitation and slavery that is now far more widespread than ever before in history. Let's move forward together, with our eyes fixed on Jesus, who has faithfully led and empowered me to take steps that I would never have imagined, all with His peace that passes all understanding that He gives as we pray. Let's walk in the Lord's power and peace as we boldly advocate for the protection of girls.

My declaration: *I am an advocate for girls, to do whatever I can to protect them from the very real threat of sexual exploiters and traffickers who masquerade as their friends or boyfriends in every community. I am also an ambassador of Jesus who offers light to dispel darkness. I extend help and hope to daughters and granddaughters who are not armed with the information and support they need to make wiser decisions to protect themselves.*

Please join me!

# Learn to Influence

# 4

# Scientific Influence Models Made Simple

## Our Responsibilities

Children are a gift from God to welcome and nurture. They need love, training, and help. Parents, extended family members, mentors, teachers, the church ... and all members of each child's world have a God-given responsibility for their well-being.[88] As babies, they are totally dependent on us for every need.

As they grow up, we continue to have the responsibility to provide, protect, teach, discipline, and love them while at the same time giving them increasing responsibility for their own decisions and actions. During their tween and teen years, their desire for independence peaks. Our effectiveness to *tell them* what to do decreases and the necessity for our *effective influence* increases. They naturally long to assert their individuality as they grow closer to adulthood. Yet our responsibilities do not change; but our methods must change.

With each birthday, we must shift and adjust the ways that we continue to shape their character. So, how do we effectively influence them for their good while respecting their need for growing independence? Also, how can we reach a generation for whom the "stakes have never been higher" and our "silence is deafening" because moments to speak "become messed-up and missed opportunities"?[89]

To begin our exploration of influence, let's define what it is.

- the capacity to affect the character, development, beliefs, attitudes, motivations, or behavior of someone
- to impact, guide, shape
- to sway, change, persuade
- to advise

Influence takes many different forms depending on the motivation of the person who seeks to influence another. Some want to persuade people to buy their product for a company's economic gain, which may or may not benefit the people who buy the product. Others may desire to impact people to adopt their social, political, or religious views for the influencer's own goals, power, and control, or to truly benefit their audience.

The predominant efforts to influence us are through the advertising and public announcements that assault us throughout each day. A basic understanding of some theories and methods, and of those messages' clout to influence people, will educate us for this journey toward becoming a positive influence in girls' lives.

Each model of influence is *explained simply*, and then is evaluated with our goals for girls in mind. Stick with me in this research summary. Together let's unearth gold nuggets in the scientific mire.

**Automatic Reactions**

Robert Cialdini, Ph. D., an experimental social psychologist and professor at Arizona State University, has studied influence through laboratory trials and by reviewing other studies. He also has applied to be a new employee in several companies to receive sales training. [90]

He has identified six fundamental psychological principles that produce an automatic subconscious willingness to say yes without thinking first, which not only shorten our decision-making process but also can be used manipulate us.

Our need to use these shortcuts is more prevalent now than ever before because of the accelerating pace of life, information, and decisions.[91] But when we understand the way the principles function, we become prepared to resist their potential control in marketing or potential sexual exploitation.

Because of these automatic reactions, behavior can be predictable, reports Cialdini. For example, when someone asks us for a favor, studies have found that the person will be more successful at getting others to say yes when they give a reason, even a flimsy one.[92] "May I go first in line to make a copy because I'm in a hurry?"

Another predictable response is when something is more expensive; we assume it is more valuable. Cialdini relates the example of turquoise jewelry sales that became brisker when the price was doubled rather than lowered, even though it was of poor quality.[93]

Automatic responses are learned indirectly while we are young. "With proper execution, the exploiters need hardly strain a muscle," Cialdini explains. "All that is required is to trigger the great stores of influence that already exist, without the appearance of manipulation."[94]

Here his six automatic principles are shared briefly.

### Consistency

"The desire for consistency is a central motivator of our behavior. It is strong enough to compel us to do what we ordinarily would not do, often causing us to act in ways that are clearly contrary to our own best interests," Cialdini explains.[95] "In most circumstances consistency is valued and adaptive."

We associate logic, stability, and honesty with consistency. But we can be taken advantage of when a person misuses our inner desire to do what is consistent with what we have said, pledged, or promised; we feel trapped and obligated to do things that we would normally never want to do. For example, the statement "I believe in you" could be manipulated to get the one who said it to do unpleasant or immoral things the other person requests.

## Reciprocation

We usually want to repay whatever another person has provided us. "People whom we might ordinarily dislike can greatly increase the chance that we will do what they wish merely by providing us with a small favor prior to their requests," Cialdini says.[96]

Sometimes girls face a dangerous use of the reciprocation rule. Guys will shower them with expensive gifts and then later, after establishing trust and love, ask them for a favor. For instance, a guy may request that his "girlfriend" earn money by working at a strip club, saying something like: "Just this once, I know the owner. I need money to pay my bills. I spent too much on you because I love you so much."[97] The girl feels internal discomfort and shame, but she agrees because of reciprocation. Cialdini reminds us, "The rule says that favors are to be met with favors; it does not require that tricks be met with favors."[98]

## Social Proof

One way that "we use to determine what is correct is to find out what other people think is correct," Cialdini teaches. "Usually, when a lot of people are doing something, it is the right thing to do. But we can be fooled by partial or fake evidence."[99] We are most vulnerable to this when we are unsure of ourselves in unclear situations, when we are with strangers, and/or when those around us are like us in some way. Our best defense is to identify inaccurate information and respond only after thinking for ourselves.

## Liking

Cialdini uses the at-home sales party to illustrate this principle. Each guest's purchase gives the friend who invited them a percentage of the sales. "The strength of that social bond is twice as likely to determine product purchase as is preference for the product itself," Cialdini writes.[100]

Liking is not limited to at-home sales parties but is used in various ways: charities get neighbors to canvas for donations; sales use a good-looking celebrity; and others use flattery and compliments. We need to mentally stop and concentrate on the product or request to separate from our liking reaction. Teen girls are hungry to receive flattery and compliments from guys, which make them vulnerable to this automatic reaction.

## Authority

Experiments have shown that people automatically react to requests made by those in authority because of their position or title, or because of signs of authority, such as a uniform, badge, or suit with tie. There is "a deep-seated sense of duty to authority within us all," Cialdini says.[101] Since we were trained as children that obedience to authority is right, we react rather than think.

This becomes a problem when a person in authority is wrong or when someone purposely deceives with the trappings of authority. We need to use heightened awareness of authority power. Usually authority figures are trustworthy but can make errors for which we need to be alert. Also, exploiters don't deserve automatic deference, especially when they try to establish their truthfulness on minor issues before lying about the major so-called facts.

## Scarcity

When searching the airlines online to plan a trip, certain low-priced flights are marked with the message "only two seats left." We feel an inner urgency to make the reservation right away. "The idea of potential loss plays a large role in human decision making," explains Cialdini.[102] Limited-numbers and deadline tactics are common for increasing sales.

This is also true for teens who will "sneak, scheme, and fight to resist attempts at control."[103] This principle can make a daughter fall more deeply in love with a guy of whom her parents say is no good. It is important to establish values when they are younger, and when they are teens, give advice rather than outright banning a relationship, which could have the opposite effect.

## Summary

"The problem comes when something causes the normally trustworthy cues to counsel us poorly, to lead us to erroneous actions and wrongheaded decisions," Cialdini says.[104] In responding to requests for a yes or no answer, we need to be alert, not relying on automatic subconscious responses. "I am at war with the exploiters—we all are," declares Cialdini.[105]

## Systematic Process

The systematic process appeals to logic and reason, such as in a lecture or documentary. This solid form of influence attempts to objectively indicate the better decision or action. A speaker, for example, evaluates the pros and cons.[106] Problems arise with this process when the presentation is prepared by someone who has a biased or harmful agenda; the resulting decision would be purposely skewed. Also, the use of logic does not speak to the emotional part of a person where resistance to the message may be stronger than in the cognitive processes, as in the case of girls whose hearts are fixed on being loved by a guy.

## Heuristic Method

The heuristic method aims to aid others in discovering something about their habits or emotions that needs to be changed; the audience is guided into self-discovery and given the choice to make changes. This employs the principles of the automatic reactions reviewed earlier.[107] But the temptation to manipulate results is still present; for example, when a product is pushed that is linked with common human desires such as being happy, popular, or sexy. How many ads can you recall that include images of people loving, laughing, kissing, hugging, and enjoying one another? Many successful ads for medications, beverages, beauty products, clothing, sports, and others quickly come to mind.[108]

## Rhetorical Method

The Greek philosopher Aristotle promoted rhetoric, which is based on the concepts of truth and justice, the ability to argue both sides of the issue, using objective proofs, credibility, reason, and emotions. This makes it an excellent method when used as it was designed.[109] But with truth and justice now being considered relative concepts by most people, this method loses its value. Who are the credible influencers we can believe and put our trust in? This requires mature judgment and understanding, which young girls may lack.

**Attribution Theory**

This theory persuades by using quotes from a person or by circumstances that would support the cause.[110] Although some attribution is a solid basis for a decision, it is highly susceptible to being selective in favor of the communicator's goals. Examples include: Does it mean that one shampoo is the best choice just because a football player says it is great? Is the popularity of a certain idea a reliable indicator that it is wise or good? Caution is needed here.

**Conditioning Theory**

Conditioning leads a person to take certain actions without direct commands but with someone's repeated positive emotional messages. A well-known proverb relates it this way: "You catch more flies with honey than you do with vinegar." This theory asserts that a new self-directed behavior can be formed when the influencer offers frequent compliments, praise, affection, and approval.[111] Obviously, this could be used for the benefit or for harmful manipulation of a person, especially when, for example, girls are hungry for affirmation and love.

**Cognitive Dissonance Theory**

Leon Festinger's theory asserts that human beings strive for mental consistency; we are uncomfortable with thoughts that clash. Therefore, influencers aim to raise the audience's discomfort so that they choose to change their minds by evaluating the cost-to-reward ratio.[112] For instance, a patient must weigh whether the side effects of a medication cost (harm) more, or less, than its rewards (benefits)?

A positive example would be girls who, after a presentation of victims' stories, in written, oral, or video format, become uncomfortable when they realize the serious dangers associated with the ways they develop relationships with guys at school, the mall, or online. Sadly, some may choose not to change but ignore the real risks by labeling them improbable because they believe the cost to their social life seems too great.

**Functional Theory**

This theory aims to increase external rewards, understanding, and a sense of self-control. For example, accumulating points on a credit card encourages us to make more credit purchases so that we are rewarded with air miles for our next trip.[113] This theory also is used for healthy parenting influence. Rather than punishment, incentives are promised to form a new habit or improved behavior. This gives both parents and children a new sense of understanding of the situation, and the children learn and enjoy self-control. Rewards need to be adjusted to be age-appropriate.

## Narrative Transportation Theory

This theory uses storytelling to capture our attention profoundly so that we find ourselves vicariously taking on the main character's role and situation. Afterwards, that character's thoughts and feelings occupy our minds to the extent that our attitudes and intentions are likely to be affirmed or to be changed to resolve or prevent a similar challenge in our own lives. The plot of a short story, book, television program, or movie can have this effect when we identify with the story.[114]

As in the case of the cognitive dissonance theory discussed earlier, true personal narratives of young women can be powerful for influencing girls. An application of this theory also could be skits or dramas in which the girls act out and actively experience narratives in which they are vicariously lured and trapped by exploiters.

## Social Judgment Theory

This theory first evaluates an audience's latitude of acceptance, which means how far they might be willing to move from their current position without completely rejecting the new idea being presented. Then a message is designed to fall near their opinion but without crossing into their realm of rejection. Change would be sought but without much resistance and with greater likelihood of acceptance.[115] Girls, for example, might outright reject the idea of completely giving up their access to social networks online just to protect themselves, so detailed instructions could be delivered on how to better protect themselves from the real risk of internet predators.

## Force

A group of influence models employ force. They include physical restraint, violence, unfair bargaining, forced contracts, misuse of authority, emotional manipulation, deception, fraud, and coercion through threats of violence to loved ones. These methods are highly effective because they eliminate others' rights to speak, to choose, to be safe, and to be fully human. Abusers, exploiters, traffickers, slave traders, criminals, and dictators use them.[116] To protect girls from predators, we must reject these methods but use methods that respect the image of God engraved in each heart by honoring her voice, body, and freedom.

## Crucial Conversations

The groundbreaking book *Crucial Conversations,* a New York Times bestseller in 2002, still offers excellent "tools for talking when the stakes are high."[117] Detailed instructions are given on how to handle key conversations in our business or personal lives. The authors define a crucial conversation as one where "opinions vary, the stakes are high, and emotions run strong."[118] This clearly fits the description for our potentially influential conversations with girls on the imminent dangers of exploitation, together with our deep desire that they choose to make wiser choices in their social lives.

The conversation, or a presentation to a group of girls, requires preparation, based on questions formulated by the authors: (1) What do I want? What do I not want? (2) Am I tempted to be silent or use violent words? Is the other person? To avoid that, how can I establish mutual respect and purpose? Do I need to apologize? (3) What are the facts, the essential issue? (4) Can I confidently express my views? (5) Will I listen to the other's views? Am I willing to paraphrase what I hear the other say to check for understanding? Am I ready to actively explore her/their views? (6) Will I look for where we agree? (7) How will decisions be made? For more details about these questions, the book is a valuable tool that includes sample conversations.

**Elaboration Likelihood Model**

ELM was developed by Richard E. Petty and John Cacioppo. It compares the processing routes of a message and how each route affects attitude change. Central to their findings is that the cognitive route is more likely to affect enduring, stable attitude change.

But, the cognitive route requires greater effort to persuade the audience than using a more attractive emotional route. For the cognitive route to bring about the desired change, the quality of the argument must be well-planned and strong enough to make understanding easy, to promote thought, and to fit the audience.

Petty and Cacioppo found that attitude changes are less enduring and more subject to errors in judgment when using emotional processing.[119] Our goal for girls is that they adopt enduring, stable attitude and behavioral changes. Therefore, we must seek to stimulate cognitive reflection with our influential messages.

**Online Persuasion**

Web psychologist Nathalie Nahai integrates and applies the science of persuasion to instruct people for their design, content development, and marketing through websites, images, videos, and social media. Much of the same information reviewed here in this chapter was collected and organized in her book for those who aim to influence online. Her book includes a detailed index, clear charts that condense the content well, and highlighted suggestions for application, all of which facilitates the effective use of this source. She also thoroughly covers the need to know the audience, its culture, emotional state, and gender; the psychology of colors; the science of eye tracking; and the effectiveness of storytelling.[120]

With people's increasingly fragmented attention, she says we need to "deliver the solutions to their problems in a frictionless way. Although we'd like to think we're rational, it is our fast, automatic system that's in charge."[121] Nahai covers the same automatic reactions reviewed earlier.[122]

## Integrated Ethical Framework

British researcher Johanna Fawkes expresses her concern that an integrated ethical framework is absent from most influence models. She declares that "the specter of [public relations and advertising] persuasion has grown more malevolent and more powerful."[123] Our motive is key to the effective and moral use of influence. Our messages for girls, who are already being shaped by the media and culture as they seek to understand life and love, require that our efforts be free of manipulation, exploitation, and injustice.

As we reflect on all the scientific models just reviewed, we recognize that efforts to influence carry with them much responsibility and require much thought and preparation. The question remains: How do we overcome the negative manipulative media influence on girls while at the same time have an effective positive influence to protect girls?

Let's investigate the models found in God's Word.

# 5

# Exploring Biblical Models of Influence

God the Creator is perfectly wise and the master of healthy influence, which He employs for the benefit of His Creation. His purpose for our lives is "to know God and enjoy Him forever."[124] *To know Him* requires that He reveal Himself to us. The Lord has revealed Himself through Creation, which shows forth His "invisible qualities—His eternal power and divine nature—[they] have been clearly seen."[125] Also, God has revealed Himself through direct interactions with people throughout history as recorded in the Bible. Preeminently, God is revealed through the earthly life of Jesus the Christ, who is God become flesh,[126] who is "the radiance of God's glory and the exact representation of His being, sustaining all things by His powerful word."[127]

*To enjoy a relationship with Him* necessitates that He influence us to freely choose to be in relationship with Him or not. All of God's revelation is recorded in the inspired and infallible words of the Bible. There we observe His methods of influence.

**Free Will**

The power to decide and act as we choose is called free will. We were given the gift of freedom of choice by our Creator. We choose to love or not, obey or not, and believe or not. This gift reveals His attitude toward the concept of influence. Rather than take absolute control over our every move, decision, and word, He created us for choice. What if love were imposed through another's control of us?

Think about a puppet. The hand that controls it creates the illusion of love by moving the puppet's hands to its mouth to blow a kiss to the audience. Even the friendly smile on its face has been pasted or painted on. The friendly voice belongs to someone else behind the curtain. On the other hand, God's creation of human beings included the desire for a truly loving relationship, which He knew cannot be forced. Love flourishes in the freedom to choose.

"Any persuasive effort which restricts another's freedom to choose for or against Jesus Christ is wrong," says Dr. Emory A. Griffin, a Christian communications specialist. "No one likes to be manipulated. 'Do unto others as you would have them do unto you'. Always respect the other's right to freely choose to say no."[128] He adds that with true love the persuader cares more about the welfare of the other person than about self. The appeal is made in a manner that respects the human rights of other people. Jesus Christ is our example of this.[129]

The story of the rich young ruler illustrates God's attitude toward choice.[130] The young man approached Jesus to ask what he must do to obtain eternal life. Jesus responded by saying he must obey the commandments; the man claimed to be perfect. Jesus discerned that it was the love of wealth that kept the rich man from loving God with his whole heart, which is the sum of all God's law.[131]

Therefore, Jesus told the man to sell his possessions, to give all the money to the poor, and to follow Him so that he would have treasure in heaven. The rich young ruler chose to walk away sadly rather than to have a heart-to-heart relationship with the Lord. Jesus did not run after him to try to convince him. He did not offer to compromise what He required of the man. He respected the man's freedom of choice. So, Jesus turned His attention back to the disciples and crowd to resume teaching them.

Principle: The foundation of effective influence is free will and excludes manipulation, coercion, and force.

## Questions

Thoughtful questions have been used by God throughout history to encourage reflection and promote possible changes in an individual's attitudes and behavior. Has anyone ever posed a question to you that kept echoing in your mind until you decided to take new steps or to make an attitude adjustment?

Sometimes my thoughtful husband will pose a question that requires reflection, not a simple question that requires only a yes or no answer. After mulling over the question that reveals his viewpoint without pushing it, I often come back to him with new perspective on the issue at hand. I find that I am more likely to hear him this way than if he were to put pressure on me.

The book of Job is an excellent example of this method of influence by God. After losing everything he had—children, livestock, and health—Job found no consolation from his wife's angry words or his friends' imperfect theological and accusatory ramblings.

He longed for an audience with God to present his case and to understand the reason God allowed the catastrophes to enter his righteous life.

In chapter 38 of the book of Job, the Lord answered him out of the storm, not with answers but with questions that continued nonstop until the end of chapter 41. Some of God's questions include: "Where were you when I laid the earth's foundation?" (38:4) "Have you ever given orders to the morning, or shown the dawn its place?" (38:12) "Do you give the horse his strength, or clothe his neck with a flowing mane?"

(39:19) "Will the one who contends with the Almighty correct Him?" (40:1) "Would you discredit My justice? Would you condemn Me to justify yourself?" (40:8) "Can you pull in the leviathan with a fishhook or tie down his tongue with a rope?" (41:1).

Job's humble reply to the Lord showed a changed attitude: "I know that you can do all things; no plan of yours can be thwarted. You asked, 'Who is this that obscures My counsel without knowledge?' Surely, I spoke of things I did not understand, things too wonderful for me to know.... Therefore, I despise myself and repent in dust and ashes" (42:1-6). The Lord then told Job's "friends" that He was angry with them for speaking inaccurately about His character. Job was directed to pray for them after they had offered burnt offerings, which he did with new humility. The Lord graciously promised to prosper Job again, this time with double his former blessings.

How would Job have responded had God lectured him or argued with him? That is a good question to ponder.

Principle: Thought-provoking questions encourage reflection and effectively promote possible changes in an individual's attitudes and behavior.

**Suffering**

Human suffering can be a motive for change. Sometimes we suffer because of our own harmful decisions. Often, we suffer because we live in a broken world and others' hurtful actions affect us. This includes all forms of suffering, such as economic, physical, and emotional. Suffering is *not* a creation of God. Suffering is the consequence of sin.

Sin is the natural human condition of being selfish, seeking our own desires and benefits over and against those of others. Also, sin is being rebellious against and independent from God and His law, which He created with our benefit in mind. This is summarized by Jesus: "'Love the Lord your God with all your heart and with all your soul and with all your mind.' This is the first and greatest commandment. And the second is like it, 'Love your neighbor as yourself.' All the Law and the Prophets hang on these two commandments."[132]

Love means value, honor, respect, deep affection, devotion, and consideration of another's feelings and needs. No one loves perfectly, so we suffer. Remember, God does not cause us to suffer. Yet He has chosen suffering to shape us if we allow Him. The Psalmists tell us that the Lord cares about the brokenhearted, the poor, and the sick,[133] and that He wants to draw us close to Himself and to redeem our suffering for growth.[134]

Parents, at times, must allow their children, especially as they are growing up, to learn from the consequences of their poor decisions that ignore sound advice and teaching. Complete control of children is impossible and undesirable as God shows by His refusal to control us like puppets so that we elect to love Him.

The lives of Jacob, Joseph, and Moses are some of the examples in which God shaped them through hardship.[135] Each started his life with selfish pride, which led him to make poor choices, but after suffering the consequences, each finished his life humble and devoted to fulfilling God's will to bless others.

The parable known as the Prodigal Son, which was told by Jesus, demonstrates the same.[136] A selfish younger son demands his inheritance before his father's death. Although it is an improper request, his father bestows those funds upon him. The son promptly runs off and "squanders his wealth in wild living."[137]

With a famine and no money remaining, the son seeks work and is offered a job feeding pigs. In the slime of the sty and with his stomach rumbling, he comes to his senses and resolves to return home to confess his sins and to beg to be a hired worker on the property. The compassionate father glimpses the son's return from afar and runs to embrace and kiss him. After hearing his son's confession and declaration that "I am no longer worthy to be called your son,"[138] the father rejects his son's offer to labor and honors him with a robe, ring, sandals, and banquet to celebrate that he "was lost and is found."[139] How beautiful to observe a life transformed through suffering!

Principle: Although pain and grief result from the consequences of bad choices, people can pray to the Lord that their own suffering or that of others will influence them to grow in healthy ways.

**Truth in Love**

Influence often involves presenting advice, data, warnings, examples, cost/benefit analysis, and truth. Those are most effective when the person sharing that information is trustworthy and does so with love, not with selfish or malicious motives. Our trustworthy and loving Creator has proclaimed truth throughout the ages to influence us for our own benefit. For those who do not choose to love Him, it is because they have not recognized His love nor accepted His truth. Yet His motives are pure for He is perfect.

God has raised up prophets, such as Isaiah, Jeremiah, Daniel, Zechariah, and many others, to be His spokespersons to expose sin and its consequences, to declare the change that is needed, and to call people into relationship with Himself for His good will and purposes.

Among the many truth-in-love messages delivered in the Bible, the prophet Isaiah declared God's missive: "'I reared children and brought them up, but they have rebelled against Me. . . . Your hands are full of blood; wash and make yourselves clean. Take your evil deeds out of my sight! Stop doing wrong, learn to do right! Seek justice, encourage the oppressed.

Defend the cause of the fatherless, plead the case of the widow .... If you are willing and obedient, you will eat the best from the land; but if you resist and rebel, you will be devoured by the sword.' For the mouth of the Lord has spoken."[140]

Jesus' encounter with the woman at the well in Sychar, Samaria, is another example of truth spoken in love, this time face-to-face by God incarnate.[141] Jesus, journeying from Jerusalem to Galilee, chose to rest at Jacob's well at noon. Most Jews would not pass through nor stop in Samaria when traveling; they would veer out of the way to avoid the Samaritans, whom they called "dogs," because of their unorthodox and syncretistic religious practices.

Jesus expressed His love through His presence in Sychar; by conversing with a woman of ill repute; by not reacting to her angry words; by offering the woman at the well "Living Water"; by not condemning her sordid history but disclosing it as fact; by teaching her about true worship; and by revealing to her His identity as the Messiah. You see, she had come to the well at noon to avoid the sneers and condemnation of the town's women who normally would fetch water in the mornings.

As Jesus' love touched the woman's heart, she grew in confidence and accepted the truth about worship and His identity, then ran to invite all the town's people to meet Jesus: "Come, see a man who told me everything I ever did. Could this be the Messiah?"[142]

After two days spent with Jesus, the people of Sychar declared: "We have heard for ourselves, and we know that this man really is the Savior of the world."[143] That truth was welcomed heartily because of the love with which it was delivered.

The inspirational author E. Stanley Jones advises, "A Christian is one who makes it easy for others to believe in God."[144] The people who influence us for good are not the people who tell us how bad we are but those who tell us whom we may become in Jesus. Love is essential for effective influence. Those who work in prevention of exploitation concur.

In the book *Hands That Heal,* the writers advise working with smaller groups of girls so that loving relationships are developed over time to build bridges of trust; this is enhanced by self-disclosure of similar challenging experiences of the leader.[145]

Principle: Truth is most effective in influencing people when it is delivered with authentic love.

## Modeling

As the sayings go, "A picture is worth a thousand words," "Talk is cheap," and "Practice what you preach." Our preeminent model is the Incarnate Word of God, Jesus Christ.[146] Parents, teachers, pastors, and others also are role models for children, tweens, teens, and young adults, especially when we are unaware that they are observing us. Words are limited in their effectiveness to influence others when a speaker's living example is absent.

Jesus' earthly life revealed the character of God in action. In the book called *The Master Plan of Teaching*, Matt Friedmann declares that in Jesus we find "the foundation for our methodology" because "lessons are better caught than taught."[147]

Reflect on how Jesus' teachings matched the life He lived. The disciples not only heard His lessons but also observed them lived out in Jesus' prayer life, character, humility, integrity, decisions, strength, service, courage, power, faith, obedience, grace, love, wisdom, endurance, sacrifice, and victory. Jesus suffered as we do and was tempted as we are, but He chose the Father's will over His human fleshly desires.[148]

Being an influential spiritual leader at home and everywhere else includes consistency between our words and actions. Because we are imperfect, that consistency involves our openly asking for forgiveness when we fail to do what is right.

Girls also need to observe adults choosing faith, love, grace, patience, humility, and integrity; dependence on the Holy Spirit; learning and growing through Bible study, prayer, and experiences;[149] guarding ourselves against harm online; and defining healthy boundaries for our own relationships.[150] Those are essentially God's desires for all followers. Being an influence means being authentic so that our faith and actions together increase our credibility.

Peer groups also can be valuable sources of influence *when a set of values with a clear purpose have been established,* declares Bennett, who founded the community-based girls' groups called Best Friends and Diamond Girls. Sound decision-making about relationships, sexuality, drugs, alcohol, and education and career planning is her goal. The message is "self-respect through self-control." Bennett has witnessed many safer, wiser, transformed lives over the past three decades.[151]

The authors of *Hands That Heal* agree: "One of the marks of a great teacher is the willingness to afford students the opportunity to learn from each other."[152]

Principle: Being true to our words with our actions increases the effectiveness of our influence as well as allowing empowered peers to be influential.

**Storytelling**

A story at bedtime has long been a special treat for children. Many adults experience getting wrapped up in the plot of a book or a drama. Stories are powerful tools to communicate history and persuasive messages as well as to entertain and virtually transport us on adventures.

Ancient records reveal that stories have been a favored form of communication throughout the ages, such as the stories narrated in the Old Testament. Parables, which are short stories used to illustrate a spiritual lesson, were frequently told by Jesus.

Today, stories still communicate well. Pastor Avery Willis, Jr. says that for those under 25 years of age, well-delivered stories make messages "stick," which means the hearers can easily remember, interpret, apply, and share the story. Being "sticky" is now essential because young people are exposed to an overwhelming number of internet and media messages, which results in a "nonstick coating" on "boring" messages. Sticky stories touch the emotions; use the senses and imagination; and deliver a concrete, credible, and simple message.[153]

Pastor Matt Friedman concurs, "The goal is to 'drive home' a point by relating the abstract or propositional to something with which people can more readily identify."[154]

When the prophet Nathan came to confront King David of his sins, he wisely decided to tell a story. The king had made poor choices: to stay at the palace rather than going to war with his troops as normal; to gaze from his roof to another roof where a beautiful woman was bathing, who probably expected all men to be on the battlefield; to misuse his power as king to request that woman named Bathsheba come to the palace; to commit adultery as a married man with a married woman; to plot to have her husband Uriah return from the battle to sleep with her to cover up her pregnancy conceived with David; and to order that Uriah be placed on the frontline so that he would be killed since Uriah had refused to sleep with his wife because he rejected to have pleasure while his fellow soldiers were at war.[155]

Nathan told King David a parable about a poor man who had one sheep that was precious to him and a rich man who had many sheep. When a visitor came to the rich man's house, he chose to take the poor man's sheep to prepare the meal rather than one of his many sheep.

Upon hearing the story, David "burned with anger" against the rich man, saying, "The man who did this deserves to die! He must pay for that lamb four times over because he did such a thing and had no pity."[156] Nathan replied, "You are the man!" and delivered God's words of judgment against David. The humbled king confessed his sins, and the prophet assured him of God's forgiveness but that he would still have to the live with the natural consequences of his sins.

The king's response would likely have been anger and rejection had Nathan only enumerated David's grave transgressions.

Jesus frequently told parables. The NIV Study Bible charts 40 parables in total.[157] The parable of the Prodigal Son, which was told earlier, is one of the most well-known. All Jesus' parables communicated the truth of life in the Kingdom of God through memorable brief plots.

A good example is the well-known parable of the Good Samaritan.[158] A religious expert in God's Law tried to test Jesus with a question, "What must I do to inherit eternal life?"[159]

Jesus questioned him about the Law, and the religious man answered correctly that we are to love the Lord with everything and to love our neighbors as ourselves. Jesus ordered him to do all that to have eternal life.

But that was unsatisfactory for the man. He wanted the word "neighbor" defined, so Jesus told this parable. A man was traveling when robbers took his clothes and beat him until he was nearly dead. A priest and a religious man both encountered the beaten man but chose to avoid him by crossing to the other side of the road. A Samaritan, an ethnic group despised by the Jews, took pity on him, cared for his wounds, took him to an inn to rest, and generously paid for his stay there, promising to return to see if more was needed.

Wisely, Jesus asked the man, "Which of the three do you think was a neighbor to the man who fell into the hands of robbers?"[160] The man answered correctly that the one who had mercy on the beaten man was a neighbor.

This truth challenged his prejudice against Samaritans whom the expert had assumed would never have a hope for eternal life. Everyone we come across each day is our neighbor, a much broader and compassionate definition than the man had heard or lived out before.

Amanda Hontz Drury, a youth leader for 15 years and now a university professor, researched the role and function of testimony in adolescent ministry.[161] Testimony is a form of storytelling; it is a narrative of events that were seen and/or heard by a witness.

Drury discovered that people's testimonies "were not just describing the past; people were being changed as they spoke . . . not just the speaker . . . those receiving the testimony were also being formed."[162] Her studies also revealed that adolescence is developmentally an ideal time to share and to hear testimonies for the sake of spiritual formation. She was glad to encounter a resurgence of the use of testimony among teenagers in some churches, through which their faith was becoming authentic and deepening.[163]

Principle: Stories communicate messages more effectively for influence than do teachings and lectures because they "stick" with us.

## Conviction and Power

The type of conviction meant here is not what happens in court when someone is found guilty of a crime and is sentenced to punishment. Rather here, it is that inner feeling in our guts that raises awareness of our wrongdoing. The source of this feeling can be our God-given conscience (such as seen when Adam and Eve hid from God after disobeying God's command).[164] It can also be something that someone has said that has brought our offense to mind (such as with Jesus' parable of the Good Samaritan or with Nathan to King David, as discussed earlier), or through the work of the Holy Spirit in a Christian or on an unbeliever.

Some people ignore convicting messages which then hardens them against change, even more with each rejection of the message. Those who listen to conviction accept it as a means for growth and maturity for a healthy life.

Sharing the truth about Jesus through the power of the Holy Spirit is vital for positive influence. Christ is the radical answer and hope for this sinful world.[165] It is essential for today's girls to know that they are valuable, loved, yet sinners for whom Jesus gave His life so that they may confess their sins, receive forgiveness, and obtain freedom, power, and wisdom against the tempting traps of the enemy.

The convicting work of the Holy Spirit is the focus here, not human efforts to convict others. Conviction of guilt "is best left to the Holy Spirit," says Griffin.[166] Besides the Spirit's direct work in our lives, two other ways exist for the Holy Spirit to convict us. One, each of us can choose to invite the Holy Spirit to reveal our wrongdoings so that we may repent, change, and grow. Two is through intercessory prayer for those whom we would like to see set free from their destructive ways.

Jesus taught his disciples about the work of the Holy Spirit in the hours before he was arrested and crucified. A role of the Holy Spirit is to convict the world of guilt.[167] This is done with the hope that those convicted will repent, be guided into all truth, and give glory to Jesus.[168]

Intercessory prayer, intervening on behalf of another person(s), entreats God to work so that His good will is accomplished. The Lord hears and delights to respond to those prayers. The Old Testament is full of prayers on behalf of others, such as Abraham praying for the protection of any believers in Sodom and Gomorrah before their destruction,[169] and the prayers of the prophets Isaiah, Jeremiah, and Habakkuk for the people whom they were called by God to confront with their sins.[170]

The New Testament records the prayers of Jesus when He knew He would soon be absent from His disciples.[171] He interceded for His disciples and for all future believers that they would be joyful, unified, protected, sanctified with truth, filled with love, and empowered through the indwelling Spirit and that they later would join Him in heaven.

Prayer is essential also because of the evil spiritual attacks that attempt to destroy girls. "Unexposed, unaddressed demonic strongholds exert tremendous power," Anderson reminds us.[172] Sexual bondage must be broken through spiritual warfare prayers, along with biblical teachings about God's good purpose for sexuality, and with patiently and gently answering the questions of girls.[173] Those prayers can result in spiritual revival that "turns careless living into vital concern and exchanges self-indulgence for self-denial."[174] This would fulfill our goal that girls be safer.

Tara Kenyon, a girls' ministry leader in Panama, advises, "Trust the Holy Spirit to do the convicting and cleaning."[175]

"We as the community of faith must prayerfully challenge the community of darkness where evil reigns," declares Grant. "We cannot do it without the supernatural intervention of the King of Kings who has all the power and spiritual authority. Pray that the Lion of Judah would break the back of these evil systems that control and perpetuate this injustice, destroying millions of people's lives."[176]

Principle: Influence, using any method, can be intensified as we also intercede for the protection, wisdom, conviction, and faith of the girls in our care, class, or church, petitioning for the work of the Holy Spirit in their lives.

**Melt**

Dr. Emory A. Griffin, author of *The Mind Changers*, uses the analogy of a candle to teach about the art of Christian persuasion. Our goal is long-lasting change, which is challenging because most people have a built-in antagonism toward anyone trying to change their attitudes or behavior, he explains. Therefore, people who want to influence others are more effective, if they admit their own weaknesses. That disclosure causes "melting" in others so that they are more likely to lower their barriers. [177]

In addition, another means of "melting" others' resistance is role playing, which means encouraging someone to take on the role of someone else in a play or skit, using verbal and emotional expression with physical movements. Role playing demands total involvement and attention. Adding improvisation by the role player can also increase the effectiveness.[178]

Paradoxically, we have the most influence on people when we are the least manipulative and take time and patience to develop a trusting relationship. Then with their trust and participation, we may see change and then invest more time to support and "solidify" new attitudes and behaviors.[179]

Did Jesus use "melting"? He may not have used that word, but the concept is seen in His relationship with His disciples. He invited the disciples to witness His deep struggles and heart-wringing prayers in the Garden of Gethsemane just before He was arrested and crucified. They witnessed His decision to obey, even unto death, after praying. Thereby, His followers were influenced in how to handle the sacrificial challenges they would face later.[180]

From the beginning of His ministry, Jesus had selected twelve disciples to be with Him constantly and develop a trusting relationship with Him. Thereby, they learned to accept the ministry Jesus called them to accomplish after His resurrection and ascension.[181]

Before that, He also had sent out the Twelve and 70 other disciples to preach and heal by His authority and power, which required them to "role play," in a sense. In Jesus' name and power but acting on their own, the assignment necessitated that they speak, act, and walk, be emotionally invested, and give complete attention to their task, not simply to be observers as they had been up until then.[182]

Principle: Trusting relationships and role-playing can cause "melting," as with a candle, of people's hearts and minds so that they are more open to be influenced to change their attitudes and actions.

## Process

Christian authors advocate using a thoughtful process to create effective messages. Field and Robbins studied clinical research of message effectiveness as well as evaluated their own experiences with teenagers to enumerate the challenges of how to get teens to pay attention; make sure they understand the message; make it believable; help them to retain the message; and motivate them to respond with action.[183] Section One of their book gives steps for thinking about the message, and Section Two shows how to create a message that "sticks."

After detailing the process, the authors remind us that we don't have to be perfect communicators, just faithful ones. So, do your best, don't worry, and remember what the Apostle Paul wrote to the Corinthians, "Always give yourself fully to the work of the Lord, because you know that your labor in the Lord is not in vain."[184]

Principle: Thoughtful preparation is key for effective influence.

Whew! That is a lot to swallow and digest. It's natural to feel overwhelmed by such a review of both scientific and biblical methods of influence. So, the next chapter will boil it all down into something we can put into practice for the best potential results for the girls we care about.

# Plan for Action

# 6

# Best Practices for Influencing Girls

**Pulling It All Together**

Now, what we need is an organized summary of what we have learned about the methods of influence and then some sample plans for practical application. Foremost, before starting, it is vital to keep reminding ourselves of the *serious responsibility* to use influence *with the best outcome in mind for the girls, not for our own comfort, convenience, or benefit.* Without first reflecting on our motives and reviewing our oft-times unexamined and reactionary methods, we will not be effective and could possibly make matters worse for the girls whom we want to influence to choose new attitudes and behaviors to protect themselves from the danger of prevalent predators. Spiritual character in the areas of authenticity, humility, courage, and kindness is vital; seek growth continually to have enduring and endearing influence.[185]

What are the best practices for influencing girls, based on the analysis of the research reviewed?

The *Doors of Hope Approach* is:

- Love genuinely, encourage with sincere praise, and be a model of true wisdom.
- Establish reasonable, achievable expectations.
- Involve both their cognitive and emotional functions.
- Place girls in small groups for assignments, discussion, and sharing, when possible.
- Endorse freedom of choice, even if they reject the message and suffer the consequences of painful mistakes; our role is to minimize rejection by using the best methods, but there is no guarantee of 100 percent success.
- Formulate thoughtful questions for girls to contemplate.
- Ponder and plan persuasive messages by using the questions posed in *Crucial Conversations* by Kerry Patterson, et al[186] and in *Speaking to Teenagers* by Field and Robbins.[187]
- Assign each girl, or each group of girls, to compile the pros and cons to assess a given topic; afterward, the leader can pose thoughtful questions about their lists to

encourage continued conversation, reflection, and possible adjustments to the list.
- Narrate "sticky" stories, using oral, written, video, drama, and skits, on such subjects as (these are samples, not an exhaustive list): genuine love versus the dangers of attraction; anecdotes of girls who were exploited but escaped to warn others of predators' methods; traps set by the media's methods of persuasion; internet risks and safety.
- Minimize the use of lecture; that requires our self-discipline. Emphasize and maintain the interaction and participation of the girls.
- Equip girls to teach others what they have learned and decided.
- Found every step and plan on a solid biblical bedrock of truth.[188]

## Critical Component **Before** You Start

*Before you gather any girls, you will need to develop a written Child Protection Policy to ensure everything is safe for the girls who will be in your care.*[189] For instance, always have at least one assistant in addition to yourself for every eight girls; have background checks on each person involved with their signed permission (well-worth the cost); determine what to do when a girl shares with you or an assistant that she is currently being abused, exploited, or trafficked; meet in a lighted, comfortable, open, safe location. Think ahead and add other issues for which you would need to develop protocol for the girls' well-being.

*Also, before* you tackle the subject of exploitation, it is wise to start with a session (or a few sessions, as time permits) with the goal of knowing the girls better and allowing them to know you. Think of a subject they would enjoy sharing with one another and you, and that can lead into the next topics of meeting friends and guys and looking for love.

**Sample Plans**

The implementation of the *Doors of Hope Approach* opens doors for diverse, creative, and endless possible strategies. Even so, excellent materials are already available, which are listed in Resources; you may need to modify those resources for increased influential effectiveness.

To begin opening those *Doors of Hope* for girls, I have delineated suggested plans. Keep in mind that a series of messages will likely be required before girls choose and communicate any change of mind or act on any new attitudes. Also, *not* every element of the *Doors of Hope Approach* needs be employed in every message; balance and appropriateness are weighed for each subject with the overall effectiveness in mind.

## Title: *Social Networking, Part One*

**Goal**

- That the girls will know the risks of being online and be armed with tactics to protect themselves.

**Supplies and preparation needed**

- In a group setting, at least one woman as leader and one woman as assistant for a maximum of 20 girls who are formed into four groups. At home, a pair of relatives, or a mother and her friend, can lead their girls together.
- A board and marker; or a computer and screen or projector for Power Point slides.
- Paper and pens for girl(s).
- A print copy of a local or state news story about a girl who was exploited by someone she met online; search online or in a newspaper for this item.
- Statistics about online use by and exploitation of children and teens (see chapter 2).
- Smart phones or tablets that belong to the girls.

**Warm Up (10 mins.)**

- Say, "Please share about anyone you know or have heard about who was exploited by someone she met online." Be sure to explain: (1) "you don't need to use the girl's real name," and (2) "exploit" means to take advantage of another person in an unfair, selfish, hurtful, abusive way.

- <u>Listen</u> with compassion and empathy; keep your remarks minimal and without opinion. Thank each for sharing.
- After the stories are shared, list and go over (using a board or Power Point slides) the statistics about the use by and exploitation of children and teens online.

## Dialogue (15 mins.)

- Either you or a girl read aloud the true story found in your local or state news about exploitation that began with online contact.
- Then ask, "What could the girl in the news have done to avoid being exploited?"

## Activity (20 mins.)

- Ask, "How many of you have an app on your device designed to protect you from danger?"
- Instruct the girls (in pairs or groups), "On your device, search to find apps designed to protect tweens and teens online, then <u>write a list of 7 apps,</u> what they do, and their cost (or if they are free). Then, <u>make a list</u> of the pros and cons of using the apps.

## Closing Challenge (10 mins.)

- Ask, "How do you feel about adding one or more protective app to your device to be safer online? Why? Does anything keep you from wanting to do that? What?"

- Close with your own follow-up questions, based on their answers, to keep them reflecting more and more deeply after the session ends. Scripture: [Jesus said,] "I am sending you out like sheep among wolves. Therefore, be as shrewd as snakes and as innocent as doves" Mt 10:16.
- Prayer is a vital last step.

**Title:** *Social Networking, Part Two*

**Goal**

- That the girls will know the risks of being online and be armed with tactics to protect themselves.

**Supplies and preparation needed**

- In a group setting, at least one woman as leader and one woman as assistant for a maximum of 20 girls who are formed into four groups. At home, a pair of relatives, or a mother and her friend, can lead their girls together.
- A board and marker; or a computer and screen or projector for Power Point slides.
- Paper and pens for girl(s).

**Warm Up (10 mins.)**

- To *review the first session*, write or keyboard these sentences for them to *see as they sit down*: "Think about what you did with us last time we met. What do you remember? Do you have any questions about what you learned? Do you have any comments to share?" *(If they are reluctant or can't remember, you can ask other questions or make comments to get a brief conversation going.)*
- For *new session* discussion, "Which social networking sites are your favorites? Why?"

**Discussion (20 mins.)**

- As you share, list (on a board or through Power Point slides) the risky behaviors below, <u>asking for their feedback or questions</u> *for each risk, one at a time.*
    1. Your *location* will be known if you don't turn it off. It may be registered by some devices even when you have turned your location off. Also, your location may be seen when you are playing games, streaming a video, and using other apps since, when you download them, you give permission for your location to be seen.
    2. When you're *feeling lonely, rejected, or angry*, and you post those feelings online, you are at a higher risk of chatting with an unknown person who responds with "sympathetic and understanding" words who wants to take advantage of your mood.
    3. *Sexting* photos can be used as a threat to force you to do whatever the person you've met online demands that you do. Those pictures that you thought were for someone special can later be posted to embarrass and shame you. Also, this kind of communication is not the foundation for a healthy relationship because love is much more than sexual.

4. Chatting with someone for weeks or months, feeling that you really know him or her, and then *meeting in person*.

- Ask, "What *other* risks are you aware of?" Add them to the list . . .

## Activity (15 mins.)

- Say, "Based on the list of risks, write down the changes a girl would need to make to be safe from exploitation online for each risk listed . . ."
- Afterward, ask for volunteers (individuals) to share their answers for each risk. Thank each for sharing.

## Closing Challenge (15 mins.)

- Pose this question to think about: "How difficult would it be for you to make the changes you listed that would protect you online? Why?"
- After a quiet time for reflection, ask the girls to discuss with one another the pros and cons of making changes. Ask for volunteers to share their thoughts. Thank each for sharing.
- Close with your own follow-up questions to keep them reflecting more and more deeply as they leave the session. Scripture: "Be self-controlled and alert. Your enemy the devil prowls around like a roaring lion looking for someone to devour" 1 Pt 5:8.
- Prayer is a vital last step.

## Title: *Predators' Schemes and Traps, Part One*

**Goal**

- That the girls will know the schemes and traps of predators and will create ideas for how to avoid becoming ensnared like a fly on a spider web.

**Supplies and preparation needed**

- In a group setting, at least one woman as leader and one woman as assistant for a maximum of 20 girls who are formed into four groups. At home, a pair of relatives, or a mother and her friend, can lead their girls together.
- A board and marker; or a computer and screen or a projector for Power Point slides.
- Computer, HDMI cord, and screen for viewing videos.
- Paper and pens for girl(s).
- Videos about girls who were trapped or nearly trapped by predators at school and at work. (The story of Theresa Flores, who was trapped at school, can be found on YouTube "Human Trafficking: A Survivor's Story by HLN." The other is "Chosen" by Shared Hope International about a girl trapped at work.)
- List of the statistics about exploitation and trafficking (see chapter 2).

### Warm Up (10 mins.)

- Ask, "Where are safe places to meet guys and new friends? How do you know they are safe?"
- Have volunteers give their opinions. Keep your responses minimal and free of opinion. Thank each for sharing.

### Videos and discussion (35 mins.)

- Show the two videos that portray girls being trapped by guys they met at school and at work.
- After viewing the videos, allow the girls to make comments and ask questions.
- Then ask and assign, "What are some changes girls would need to make to avoid being trapped like a fly on a spider's web, based on what you saw? Now, please make a list with your group of your ideas for being safer."
- Ask for ideas to be shared. Thank each for sharing.
- Show the statistics about exploitation and trafficking. Listen, if any have comments.

### Closing Challenge (15 mins.)

- Pose this question to think about, "Those changes you talked about may change your social life. Do you think your safety is more important or is meeting new friends *as you do now* more significant? Why?" Listen without expressing comment or opinion.

- Close by telling them to keep reflecting deeply as they leave the session. Scripture: "Be self-controlled and alert. Your enemy the devil prowls around like a roaring lion looking for someone to devour" 1 Pt 5:8.
- Prayer is a vital last step.

## Title: *Predators' Schemes and Traps, Part Two*

**Goal**

- That the girls will know the schemes and traps of predators and will create ideas for how to avoid becoming ensnared like a fly on a spider web.

**Supplies and preparation needed**

- In a group setting, at least one woman as leader and one woman as assistant for a maximum of 20 girls who are formed into four groups. At home, a pair of relatives, or a mother and her friend, can lead their girls together.
- A board and marker; or a computer and screen or a projector for Power Point slides.
- Paper and pens for girl(s).
- Photocopies of victims' accounts: have a different one for each group, one copy for each girl of her group's story (look in Resources).

**Warm Up (10 mins.)**

- Say, "Please take time to silently read the true reports each group has been handed. Circle the name of each person in the true story."

**Activity (15-20 mins.)**

- Instruct, "Your assignment is to create a 5-minute skit with your group based on the report you have just read. Your director is to be the person whose birthday is closest to today. The director is to assign each girl in her group the part of a person in the report, even if it is the part of a guy. Condense the report as needed to use the most important conversations of the report to fit the 5 minutes you will have to perform. Each girl needs to underline her part on her copy and cross out what will be left out. You may hold your papers in your hands when you are performing your skit for all of us. Please be sure to show your character's emotions in your acting. You now have 15-20 minutes to plan and practice." (These steps could be listed on the board or a Power Point slide.)

## Activity (20 mins.)

- Each group performs their skit while the others watch quietly and politely. (If more time is needed for practice and performance, this lesson can be resumed during the next session.)

## Closing Challenge (15 mins.)

- Pose this question to *think about*, "How would you feel if you were the victim in each skit?"
- Close with telling them to keep reflecting deeply on the victims in the skits as they leave the session. Scripture: [Jesus said,] "Watch out that no one deceives you [leads you astray]" Mt 24:4.
- Prayer is a vital last step.

## Title: *Predators' Schemes and Traps, Part Three*

**Goal**

- That the girls will create ideas for how to avoid becoming ensnared like a fly on a spider web.

**Supplies and preparation needed**

- In a group setting, at least one woman as leader and one woman as assistant for a maximum of 20 girls who are formed into four groups. At home, a pair of relatives, or a mother and her friend, can lead their girls together.
- A board and marker; or a computer and a screen or a projector for Power Point slides.
- Paper and pens for girl(s).
- A complete list of ways predators trap girls.
- The book *Crucial Conversations* (see Resources) is needed to prepare for this session. Focus mostly on chapter 10, but the entire book is needed to fully understand the principles, and many examples of conversations are given throughout the book to make the ideas clearer.

*The following four steps are completed during preparation time, to set your heart right before you meet with the girls.*

- o Start with Heart. Ask yourself: What do I really want for me? for others? for the relationship? What do I not want? How should I go about

getting what I really want and avoiding what I don't want?
- Learn to Look. Prepare to look for when the conversation becomes crucial with safety issues: Am I going to silence or violence? Are others?
- Make It Safe. How can I establish Mutual Purpose and Mutual Respect? Do others believe I care about their goals in this conversation? Do they trust my motives? Commit to seek mutuality. Recognize purpose. Brainstorm strategies. Am I ready to apologize when appropriate? Will I contrast to fix misunderstanding (i.e., "I'm sorry. I didn't mean to communicate . . . I meant to say . . .")?
- Master My Story. How can I stay in dialogue when I feel angry, scared, or hurt? Recognize my feelings. Then stick to the facts, and avoid Victim, Villain, and Helpless Stories.

*The other three steps are prepared and then put into practice during the session's use of dialogue*: 1) State My Path; 2) Explore Others' Paths; and 3) Move to Action.

**When meet with girls, leader starts a dialogue (10 mins.)**

- Present <u>a complete list</u> of all the ways predators operate and briefly explain those that were not reviewed in the previous sessions. (Learn this from reading news articles and books and by reviewing Resources.)

- State that ALL girls are at risk of being exploited unless they know the traps and unless they change their decisions and actions about how to make new friends. Also, girls are at risk because they are vulnerable.
    - Vulnerable means susceptible to injury; unprotected from danger; insufficiently defended; likely to give into persuasion or temptation
    - Give causes of being vulnerable: *normal hunger to be liked or loved; lack of information about risks; lack of confidence; feeling not understood and lonely; and by certain life experiences* (such as being an orphan or a foster child; feeling unloved by parents; being abused by parents or others; experiencing divorce of parents; running away from home; living in poverty; having a chronic illness or a disability; moving often; death of someone close).
    - Say, "Our vulnerability is seen by others even when we attempt to cover it up. Some people, instead of showing compassion for us, will take advantage of us and exploit us."

**Girls' part of dialogue (10 mins.)**

- Ask for their responses, feelings, and questions. Encourage them to speak their hearts. Listen without judgment and comment; this takes our love and patience. Remember to keep a sense of mutual purpose

and respect and to keep the conversation safe as you have prepared.
- Seek to understand what they say. Be sure to check for understanding by rephrasing what you think you hear them say. Ask follow-up questions.

**Leader's part of dialogue (5 mins.)**

- Pose this question, "How could you meet new friends and guys more safely?"

**Girls' part (10 mins.)**

- Again, listen compassionately to their answers. Keep the dialogue safe for them. Thank each for sharing.

**Closing Challenge (10 mins.)**

- Close with telling them to keep reflecting deeply on the risks, vulnerability, and the previous skits as they leave the session, and write a list of ideas for ways to avoid becoming a fly stuck on a spider's web. Tell them that they will start the next session with their lists. Scripture: "[The person] who walks in wisdom is kept safe" Pr 27:26b.
- Prayer is a vital last step.

## Title: *What is Love?*

*(First session of many that would be needed on this subject)*

### Goal

- That girls will learn about love and explore how to recognize a potentially genuine, secure, satisfying, and lifelong relationship. A study showed that 90 percent of girls dream of being married (as referenced earlier).

### Supplies and preparation needed

- In a group setting, at least one woman as leader and one woman as assistant for a maximum of 20 girls who are formed into four groups. At home, a pair of relatives, or a mother and her friend, can lead their girls together.
- A board and marker; or a computer and screen or a projector for Power Point slides.
- Computer, HDMI cord, screen to view video.
- Paper and pens for girl(s).
- Locate a video online about real love. There are many. Look online for "short Christian videos for teens about _____ (fill in the blank with words such as love, or relationships, or purity)." For this session, I recommend: http://fervr.net/videos/what-is-love.

## Warm Up (15 mins.)

- Say, "In your groups, please make a list of the qualities of a healthy marriage relationship." Have one person from each share the group's answers.
- Say, "Next write down your answers to these questions: 1. How many of you think that it is possible to have a loving marriage that lasts a lifeline? 2. How many of you would like to get married some day?" Again, they share each group's answers.

## Activity (30 mins.)

- Watch the video (3 ½ minutes).
- Ask for reactions, questions, and comments. Listen without comment or judgment. Thank each for sharing.
- Reshow the video, asking them to listen and watch for things they didn't catch the first time.
- Give each girl a piece of paper and ask her to respond to some questions (below). You will read each question aloud and allow time for them to write their responses. *Assure them that it's not a test* but time for them to reflect; it is not a problem if they can't remember these details.
    1. When did the couple first meet?
    2. How old was he when they started dating?
    3. Was there physical attraction?
    4. *Do you think* they understood what real love is before they married? Explain.

5. What activity have they shared throughout their relationship?
  6. What is the reason that caring for his wife is not a burden for him?
  7. What did he say is the source of the love that he has for her?
  8. Make a list of the qualities that *you think* the wife saw in her husband while they were dating that would have predicted that he was going to treat her so well.

- Ask for volunteers to give their answers to questions numbered 1 through 7. Listen as they share. *Only provide an answer if no one has an answer to a fact-based question; number 4 calls for an opinion so there's no need to give a correct answer there.*

## Group Activity (10 mins.)

- Say, "Get together with your groups and share your answers to question number 8. Add to your list anything new that comes up in your discussion. These will be discussed during the Warm Up of the next session."

## Closing Challenge (5 mins.)

- Give them the internet address of the video and suggest that they watch it again at home as they think about their own dreams and future. Say: "Add to your list for number 8 so that you gather more ideas about how to

*recognize a potentially* genuine, secure, satisfying, and lifelong relationship."
- Scripture: read aloud 1 Cor 13:4-7.
- Prayer is a vital last step.

**Your Turn to Create Plans**

I'm stopping here with the sample plans. The number, styles, and subjects of session plans are endless. I trust that you will research, reflect, and plan many more sessions on the subjects elaborated in the samples. Other subjects for a series of presentations could include Media Traps (i.e., how ads use our desire to be loved and our automatic reactions to sell products) and Passing It On (i.e., equip the girls to share what they have learned to effectively influence their friends).

The subject of influencing girls to protect themselves against predators' exploitations is deep and complex, so the issues and topics required to influence girls are limitless. Some ideas for plans can be found in Resources at the end of the book. Also, *Doors to Close, Doors to Open,* and its leader's guide are recommended as companions to this book.[190] Your investment in girls' lives will be well worth it. You *can* have a positive influence that saves them from entering damaging and destructive relationships.

**Testimony of a Changed Life**

Transformation is the goal for the sake of girls' safety and well-being. That transformation will take place when we leaders follow God's Word and ways of influence, together with the power of the Holy Spirit and prayer. As Romans 12:2 (NCV) says to us and our girls: "Do not be shaped by this world; instead be changed within by a new way of thinking. Then you will be able to decide what God wants for you; you will know what is good and pleasing to Him and what is perfect."

Many girls have been vulnerable and trapped by cultural expectations into a cycle of broken dreams after opening themselves sexually to guys who exploit and discard them.

Yet they can be enabled to experience an emotional and spiritual makeover that frees them to be hopeful, courageous, self-protective, healed, and restored for all the wonderful plans the Lord has for each one. And, they can share their experiences with others so that they too can be healed and self-protective.[191]

Stacy wrote an email to Andy Stanley, an effective writer, and speaker, about her transformation through his godly guidance. She shared with him that she grew up in a broken home. Her mother encouraged her to wait to have sex until she found someone she loved, but she didn't encourage her to wait until marriage. Stacy only knew that her high school friends were having sex, so she gave herself away to every boyfriend she had.

In her dorm room at college, she listened to messages online by Stanley. One night what she heard became "the moment of truth in my life and my largest milestone to this day." Stacy recognized the connection between her many sexual experiences and the numbness she had been feeling about life. She took Stanley up on his challenge to stop dating for one year and to put in writing her commitment to have no more sex until marriage.

During that year, she gradually became a sensitive person again, confessed her sins, and invited Jesus to work in her heart. At the end of the year, an acquaintance from high school contacted her and they became friends. He too was a Christian. As they talked over some months, Stacy says that she "saw the beauty of what God wanted to do through our lives."

Two years later, he asked her to marry him, which they did after one more year. She says, "Our relationship is based on friendship and faith. If it weren't for the year thing and all God changed in my heart, not only would I be incapable of loving him the way he deserves to be loved, I probably wouldn't have him at all."[192]

What an inspiration to hear how God, working through those devoted to influencing others for good, turns lives from paths of destruction into ones of healthy, satisfying, abundant life! More people are needed to reach all the girls vulnerable to abuse, exploitation, and trafficking. Will you be one of them?

# 7

# Invite Others

Most people don't know that exploitation and human trafficking is a *real threat to the daughters and young neighbors in their lives*, so they tend to ignore or reject information about it initially.[193] You and I need to use the same influence methods we've learned in this book to influence and invite parents, teachers, leaders, and pastors to join in the efforts to influence to protect girls.

We Christians are called to biblical justice, *each one* of us.[194] We together *can* accomplish the goal to minimize and to end exploitation. Justice is *not* impossible. That's because of *who* God is, because He is *always with us,* and because He *keeps His promises*. Every moment, even small steps in the direction of justice, is crucial. The anti-exploitation and anti-trafficking movement is a series of small steps by each of many people. The time is now to step out and join those of us already committed.[195]

Everyday moms Shayne Moore and Kimberly McOwen Yim encourage us to refuse to remain idle about exploitation. They wrote a book about their journey from becoming aware of the problem to becoming activists together.

Their book's forward, written by Elisa Morgan, inspires us to be like Mary of Mark 14:3-9. Mary generously poured out an expensive perfume on Jesus. Although others present criticized her, Jesus affirmed her saying, "She did what she could."[196] We each have something we *can* do. Moore and Yim suggest we start with prayer. That includes spiritual warfare prayer, intercessory prayer, and deep, constant prayer.

Steps for justice also begin with compassion for those who are suffering or are in danger of exploitation. Compassion is the motive and centerpiece of Jesus' ministry, as seen throughout the New Testament, and He calls us to follow Him as He leads.[197] So, let's reflect on our level of compassion by looking at the offering of our time, money, and conversations. What changes could we make to start influencing girls as well as influencing adults to join us?[198] You *can* do something—see the following list for suggestions—and you certainly can add to the movement by doing things you know you can do, even the little things! Be encouraged by this truth: "The movement gains momentum each time a new [person] joins."[199] Go for it in

*God's* power, wisdom, and leading, using the experiences, gifts, and talents you have been given by Him!

"Choose to face darkness. Choose to cast despair to the wayside. Choose to let God lead you above all else. Choose hope," advises Bethany Hoang of International Justice Mission.[200] "God is on the move, restoring and redeeming... We are called to live as those who, in the midst of the unbearable, in the midst of the pain, do not shrink back but rather rise up."[201]

**Suggestions**

1. Pray regularly for the girls you know and for prevention and antitrafficking ministries. Pray for traffickers and exploiters to repent. Be encouraged: "Yes, the battle against evil is great, but our God is greater. He is still performing miracles on behalf of those who put their trust in Him."[202]
2. Seek God daily. "Seeking justice doesn't begin at the door of a brothel [for example]. Seeking justice begins with seeking the God of justice."[203] Read passages in the Bible that talk about justice, such as Isaiah 61. Without roots in God, we will burn out striving in our own power.[204]
3. Have hope. "Hope is grounded in the reality of who God is and how He works in the world. God

is inviting us to join the work He is already doing."[205]
4. Give contributions to a prevention and antitrafficking group in your area. Look online.
5. Read the books and websites, and watch the videos listed in Resources.
6. Share what you have learned; use thoughtful questions, tell real life accounts of victims, and talk about news items related to this subject.
7. Keep your eyes open for *possible* victims. (A *list of possible signs*: signs of physical harm; truancy; seems disoriented or drugged; inappropriate clothing for the weather; a sudden change in attire, behavior, or possessions; malnourished; withdrawn and fearful; confident and boasting; has an older boyfriend who is controlling or gives her expensive gifts early on; the accompanying adult answers all questions for a child; inappropriate touch or rough touch; claims to be an adult but has adolescent features; identification cards are missing; lives and works in the same place; new branding, tattoos, or carvings. *Increased risk factors*: unstable home life, abused, neglected, runaway, low self-esteem, addiction, family on welfare, held in the criminal justice system, a gang member, and a victim of bullying.)[206]

8. Call the NATIONAL TRAFFICKING HOTLINE with concerns at 888-3737-888 (written this way for ease of memorization).
9. Start an education and prayer group for those you've shared with to intercede together for the girls you know; use the *Doors of Hope Approach* while teaching adults too.
10. Print helpful posters from the Homeland Security website and post them everywhere possible, especially in youth or women's restrooms.[207]
11. Together with those you've influenced, start reaching out to girls you know in small groups of six to eight, *after developing your protection protocol and preparing lessons.*
12. Persevere despite any pushback, difficulties, or criticism; this happens because the enemy doesn't want this issue brought out into the light.
13. Attend conferences about the abolition of modern-day slavery/antitrafficking.
14. Volunteer to work with a local runaway/homeless teens shelter, a recovery program, or an antitrafficking ministry. This might include clerical or other practical work.
15. Use your influence with your church leaders/pastors to start an annual Freedom Sunday with the pledge: We will not tolerate any child created by God in our neighborhood or our

sphere of influence to be trafficked, sold, or used. We will pray [supply prayer guides], give [to an antitrafficking ministry your church chooses], and communicate with others to stop this injustice locally and globally.[208]

16. Learn from local community police, educators, social workers, juvenile justice workers, mayor, city council, active citizens, et al, to find out what they know about local trafficking and what they are doing to prevent or stop exploitation. They may need education which you and your group could provide.

17. Write letters to politicians in the state government to change laws to fight trafficking more effectively, *after* you discover the laws that already exist.

# Endnotes

1. Names have been changed to protect identity.

2. Nita Belles, *In Our Backyard: A Christian Perspective on Human Trafficking in the United States* (Free River Press, 2011), 107.

3. This story can be found online and in her books. Go to www.youtube.com and see "Human Trafficking: A Survivor's Story by HLN" and other videos under her name. Look for her books too on Amazon.

4. Theresa Flores and Peggy Sue Wells, *Slave Across the Street: Blackmailed into Sex Trafficking* (Garden City, ID: Ampelon Publishing, 2007).

5. Belles, 109-110.

6. Names have been changed to protect identity.

7. Gretchen Smeltzer, "Cultivate Freedom Workshop," (speaker at GO61 Mini-Conference, The Way Church, Springfield, MO, September 9, 2017). See Resources about online protection.

8. Story condensed from Belles, 4-22. Names changed to protect identity.

9. Belles, 15; https://fightslaverynow.org/why-fight-there-are-27-million-reasons/human-trafficking-is-modern-day-slavery/defining-some-terms/, re-accessed June 11, 2018; Grant, Beth and Cindy Lopez Hudlin, eds., *Hands That Heal: International Curriculum to Train Caregivers of Trafficking Survivors,* Community-Based Edition, Part 1 (Springfield, MO: Project Rescue/FAAST, 2007), 15, 41.

10. Bethany Hoang, *Deepening the Soul for Justice* (Downers Grove, IL: IVP with International Justice Mission, 2012), 43.

11. Ibid.

12. Grant, *Hands*, 33, 41, 47.

13. Chapter 7 of www.kidslivesafe.com.

14. Ibid.

15. Ibid.

16. Ibid.

17. "The Issues: Child Sexual Exploitation – Infograph," *The National Center for Missing & Exploited Children*, accessed March 2018, re-accessed June 11, 2018. www.missingkids.com/theissues/cse/1in7. This website has many resources and much information on these issues.

18. Belles, 15.

19. "Archived NCIC Missing Person and Unidentified Person Statistics" *National Crime Information Center (NCIC)* (2014), accessed March 2018, re-accessed June 2018, https://archives.fbi.gov/archives/about-us/cjis/ncic/ncic-missing-person-and-unidentified-person-statistics-for-2014

20. "Child, Youth, and Teen Victimization" in *Child Welfare and Information Gateway* (2015), accessed March 2018, re-accessed June 2018, http://victimsofcrime.org/docs/default-source/ncvrw2015/2015ncvrw_stats_children.pdf?sfvrsn=2 (document:2015 ncvrw_stats_children.pdf)

21. "Info and Stats for Journalists: Statistics about sexual violence," NCVRC (National Sexual Violence Resource Center, 2015) accessed March 15, 2018, www.nsvrc.org/sites/default/files/publications_nsvrc_factsheet_media-packet_statistics-about-sexual-violence_0.pdf

22. "2017 Trafficking in Persons Report" (U.S. Department of State, 2017), accessed March 2018, re-accessed June 11, 2018, https://www.state.gov/j/tip/rls/tiprpt/countries/2017/271309.htm

23. "Human Trafficking by the Numbers: Fact Sheet" (Human Rights First, January 7, 2017) accessed June 11, 2018, https://www.humanrightsfirst.org/resource/human-trafficking-numbers

24. "Findings" Global Slavery Index (The Minderoo Foundation, 2018) accessed March 2018, re-accessed June 11, 2018 www.globalslaveryindex.org/findings/

25. David Batstone, *Not for Sale: The Return of the Global Slave Trade and How We Can Fight it* (New York: Harper-Collins e-books, 2007), 17. Kindle edition.

26. Ibid, 18.

27. Ibid, 269.

28. Ibid, 5-9, 104-105; also, see David Platt, *Counter Culture: Follow Christ in an Anti-Christian Age* (Carol Stream, IL: Tyndale House Publishers, 2017), 119. Kindle edition.

29. International Justice Mission, www.ijm.org; also, see Gary A. Haugen and Victor Boutros, *The Locust Effect: Why the End of Poverty Requires the End of Violence* (Oxford: Oxford University Press, 2014).

30. Batstone, 191-193.

31. Ibid, 229, 278-279.

32. Ibid, 3-4.

33. Belles, 74-75.

34. Ibid, 95.

35. Grant, *Courageous Compassion,* 152-153.

36. Ibid, 143; also, see Batstone, 3-4.

37. Joni Middleton, "Dignity Markers" (speaker at ICAP Conference, Green Lake, Wisconsin. May 21-26, 2017).

38. Elayne Bennett, M.ED., *Daughters in Danger: Helping Our Girls Thrive in Today's Culture* (Nashville, TN: Nelson Books, 2014), 147.

39. Ibid, 31, 147.

40. Eric Buehrer, *The New Age Masquerade: The Hidden Agenda in Your Child's Classroom* (Brentwood, TN: Wolgemuth & Hyatt, Publishers, Inc., 1990), 41-42.

41. Ibid, 42-50.

42. Corrie Cutrer, "The Loneliness Epidemic," *Today's Christian Woman* (December Week 3, 2014).

43. Bennett, 55, 75, 145.

44. Ibid, 61-63, 125-142.

45. Bob Hoskins and Robert D. Hoskins, "Spiritual State of the World's Children," *ABY: Attitudes & Behaviors of Youth, a Global Study* (2012), 12, 16, 18, accessed June 7, 2018, http://cdn.onehope.net/pdfs/ABY_Book.pdf

46. Jim Anderson with Heidi Karlsson, *Unmasked: Exposing the Cultural Sexual Assault* (Spokane, WA: Lifeline Ministries, 2011), 8, 79-81, 121.

47. Ibid, 2.

48. Ibid, 96.

49. Ibid, 29; also, see Platt, 124.

50. Platt, 126.

51. R. York Moore, *Making All Things New: God's Dream for Global Justice* (Downers Grove, IL: IVP Books, 2012), 43.

52. Bennett, ix-x. She cites many examples throughout her book.

53. Andy Stanley, *The New Rules for Love, Sex & Dating* (Grand Rapids, Michigan: Zondervan, 2014) 12, 15, 21-33, 120, 144; also, see Anderson, 69-70; Gary Chapman, *The 5 Languages of Love: The Secret to Love that Lasts* (Chicago: Moody Publishers, 2014), 27-36.

54. Bennett, xi-xii.

55. Jim Anderson, 59, 61, 69-70, 118, 221.

56. Bennett, xiv, 49. For details about college culture, Bennett, 1-29.

57. Andy Stanley, *Enemies of the Heart: Breaking Free from the Four Emotions That Control You* (Colorado Springs: Multnomah Books, 2011), 196, 201.

58. Smeltzer.

59. Ibid.

60. Stanley, *New Rules*, 124-125.

61. Phyllis Kilbourn, editor, *Children in Crisis: A New Commitment* (Monrovia, CA: MARC, 1996) 29-41.

62. Belles, 146-48.

63. Rachel Lloyd, *Girls Like Us, A Memoir: Fighting for a World Where Girls Are Not for Sale* (New York: Harper Perennial, 2011), 87-90.

64. Ibid.

65. Ibid.

66. Cherry Teketel Friedmeyer, "Prevention of Prostitution and Human Trafficking" (speaker at ICAP Conference, Green Lake, Wisconsin. May 21-26, 2017).

67. Jessica Pittman, "Engaging the Church: Partnership and Prevention" (speaker at ICAP Conference, Green Lake, Wisconsin. May 21-26, 2017).

68. Bennett, 65.

69. Stanley, *New Rules*, 48, 59, 60, 66.

70. Ibid, 184.

71. Ibid, 131-150, 152; also, see Jim Anderson, 209.

72. Robert S. McGee, *The Search for Significance* (Nashville, TN: W Publishing Group, 2003), 11.

73. Ibid, 19-21, 27, 115-117, 151.

74. Platt, 126, 127, 130.

75. Ibid, 128.

76. Casey Alvarez, "Opening Session" (executive director and speaker at GO61: Liberty Conference, Broadway Baptist Church, Springfield, MO, November 3-4, 2017).

77. Jim Anderson, 126-127.

78. Grant, *Courageous Compassion*, 154-155.

79. Grant, *Hands*, 67-70.

80. Bennett, xi-xiii.

81. A few samples of suggested resources: an excellent source for God's standards is Andy Stanley, *How Good is Good Enough: Since Nobody's Perfect* (Colorado Springs: Multnomah Books, 2003); a good example of denominational pamphlets is Assemblies of God Perspectives, *Relationships, Conduct & Sexuality: Keys for Building Godly Relationships* (Springfield, MO: Gospel Publishing House); a good professional curriculum, especially session 3, is www.a21.org/content/banc/go2vpc.

82. Joshua Harris, *I Kissed Dating Goodbye: A New Attitude Toward Romance and Relationships* (Sisters, OR: Multnomah Books, 1997).

83. Dr. Henry Cloud and Dr. John Townsend, *Boundaries in Dating: Making Dating Work* (Grand Rapids, MI: Zondervan, 2000).

84. Stanley, *New Rules*.

85. "William Wilberforce: Quotes," accessed November 7, 2017, https://www.goodreads.com/author/quotes/191362. William Wilberforce. William Wilberforce, whose abolition work is the subject of the 2006 movie "Amazing Grace," devoted his life to promoting the bill against slavery until it was finally passed in England.

86. Irv A. Brendlinger, *To Be Silent...Would Be Criminal: The Antislavery Influence and Writings of Anthony Benezet* (Lanhan, MD: The Scarecrow Press, Inc., 2007). Benezet wrote numerous tracts against slavery that influenced Granville Sharp, Thomas Clarkson, John Wesley, Benjamin Franklin, and many others to join the fight against slavery.

87. Shayne and Kimberly McOwen Yim, *Refuse to Do Nothing: Finding Your Power to Abolish Modern-Day Slavery* (Downers Grove, IL: Intervarsity Press, 2012). Kindle edition; also, see David Platt, *Counter Culture: Follow Christ in an Anti-Christian Age* (Carol Stream, IL: Tyndale House Publishers, 2017), 120. Kindle edition.

88. Douglas McConnell, Jennifer Orona, and Paul Stockley, eds. *Understanding God's Heart for Children: Toward a Biblical Framework* (Colorado Springs, CO: Authentic Publishing, 2007), 4-6.

89. Doug Fields and Duffy Robbins, *Speaking to Teenagers: How to Think about, Create & Deliver Effective Messages* (Grand Rapids, MI: Zondervan, 2007), 255, 314. Kindle edition.

90. Robert Cialdini, Ph.D., *Influence: The Psychology of Persuasion* (New York: Harpercollins, 2009), Introduction. Kindle edition.

91. Ibid, 3.

92. Ibid, 4.

93. Ibid, 8-9.

94. Ibid, 44-48.

95. Ibid, 16, 28.

96. A paraphrase from dialogue in the video "Chosen," which can be purchased at www.sharedhope.org/chosen; also, see Cialdini, 26.

97. Cialdini, 39.

98. Ibid, 88.

99. Ibid, 127.

100. Ibid, 160.

101. Ibid, 179.

102. Ibid, 186.

103. Ibid, 209.

104. Ibid, 210.

105. Ibid.

106. Lynn Munoz, "Systematic Model of Processing," *Life Long Learning* blog (October 13, 2013), accessed December 2016, re-accessed June 12, 2018, https://lynnmunoz.wordpress.com/2013/10/13/systematic-model-of-processing/

107. Cialdini, chapter 1.

108. Cindy Dietrich, "Decision Making: Factors that Influence Decision Making, Heuristics Used and Decision Outcomes," *Inquiries Journal 2*, no. (2010): 2-3, accessed December 2016, re-accessed June 12, 2018, www.inquiriesjournal.com/articles/180/2/decision-making-factors-that-influence-decision-making-heuristics-used-and-decision-outcomes

109. Cristof Rapp, "Aristotle's Rhetoric," *Stanford Encyclopedia of Philosophy* (February 1, 2010), accessed December 2016, re-accessed June 12, 2018, https://plato.stanford.edu/entries/aristotle-rhetoric/#means

110. Saul McLeod, "Attribution Theory," *Simply Psychology* (2012), accessed December 2016, re-accessed June 12, 2018, https://simplypsychology.org/attribution-theory.html; also, see Cialdini, chapter 5.

111. "Classical Conditioning," *Changing Minds*, accessed December 2016, re-accessed June 12, 2018, http://www.changingminds.org/explanations/theories/classical_conditioning.htm; also, see J. Anderson, 199-200.

112. Richard Culattta, "Cognitive Dissonance," *Instructional Design* (2018), accessed June 12, 2018, www.instructionaldesign.org/theories/cognitive-dissonance.html; also, see Cialdini, chapter 3.

113. Jose Hernandez, "Functional Theory of Attitudes: Explained" *The Consumer Bio World* (April 19, 2015), accessed December 2016, re-accessed June 12, 2018, www.jhernandezpro.wordpress.com/2015/04/19/functional-theory-of-attitudes-explained

114. David Nussbaum, "Narrative Transportation" *Dave Nussbaum*, accessed December 2016, re-accessed June 12, 2018, www.davenussbaum.com/blog/narrative-transportation

115. "Social Judgment Theory," *Contexts of Communication*, accessed December 2016, re-accessed June 12, 2018, www.oregonstate.edu/instruct/theory/sjt.html; also, see Smeltzer; Bennett, 95-114.

116. Shari Alexander, "Separating The Four Horsemen: Influence, Persuasion, Manipulation and Coercion" *Bringing the "Dark Arts" of Influence into the Light,* accessed December 2016, re-accessed June 12, 2018, www.shari-alexander.com/influence-persuasion-manipulation-coercion

117. Kerry Patterson, Joseph Grenny, Ron McMillan, and Al Switzler, *Crucial Conversations: Tools for Talking When the Stakes are High* (New York: McGraw Hill, 2002).

118. Ibid, 1-2.

118. "Elaboration Likelihood Model," *Changing Minds*, accessed December 2016, re-accessed June 12, 2018, www.changingminds.org/explanations/theories/elaboration_likelihood.htm

120. Nathalie Nahai, *Webs of Influence: The Psychology of Online Persuasion, Secret Strategies that Make Us Click* (Harlow, UK: Pearson Education Limited, 2017). Kindle edition.

121. Ibid, 4, 7.

122. Cialdini, chapter 1.

123. Johanna Fawkes, "Public Relations Models and Persuasion Ethics: A New Approach," *Emerald Journal of Communication Management* 11, no. 4 (2007): 313-331.

124. "Westminster Shorter Catechism," accessed March 2018, re-accessed June 12, 2018, http://bpc.org/wp-content/uploads/2015/06/d-scatechism.pdf

125. Rom 1:20.

126. Jn 1.

127. Heb 1:3.

128. Emory A. Griffin, *The Mind Changers: The Art of Christian Persuasion* (Wheaton, IL: Tyndale House Publishers, Inc., 1976), 27-30. Also, see Mt 7:12.

129. Ibid, 40; also, see 1 Th 2:3-8.

130. Mt 19:16-30; Mk 10:17-31; Lk 18:18-30.

131. Mt 22:37-40.

132. Mt 22:37-40; Jesus quoted Dt 6:5 and Lev 19:18.

133. Ps 34; 106; 147.

134. Ps 41; 103; 130.

135. Ge 27-35; Ge 37-50; Ex 1-40.

136. Lk 15:11-32.

137. Lk 15:13.

138. Lk 15:21.

139. Lk 15:32.

140. Isa 1:2, 15-20.

141. Jn 4:4-42.

142. Jn 4:29.

143. Jn 4:42.

144. E. Stanley Jones, *Victorious Living* (Nashville: Abingdon Press, 2015), 5719. Kindle edition. See the weeks numbered 39-40 that share the story of the woman at the well from John 4 to show how we are to make it easy for others to believe.

145. Grant, *Hands*, 53-70.

146. Jn 1.

147. Matt Friedeman, *The Master Plan of Teaching: Understanding and Applying the Teaching Styles of Jesus* (Wheaton, IL: Victor Books of Scripture Press Publications, Inc., 1990), 13, 49.

148. Heb 2:18; 4:14-15.

149. Barbara J. Mandley, *Parenting with a Wise Heart* (Aloha Publishing.com, 2014), 67-96.

150. Smeltzer.

151. Bennett, esp. 94-218. Her mission statement is: "Best Friends is a nationwide network of programs that is dedicated to the physical and emotional well-being of adolescents. It provides scientifically researched and developmentally sound curriculum designed for high school students. The Foundation promotes self-respect through self-control and give participants the skills, guidance, and support needed to avoid risky behavior that is destructive to relationships. In the spirit of true friendship, the Best Friends Foundation fosters positive peer groups for adolescents and creates an environment that raises aspirations and promotes achievement."

152. Grant, *Hands*, 95.

153. Avery T. Willis, Jr. and Mark Snowden, *Truth that Sticks: How to Communicate Velcro Truth in a Teflon World* (Colorado Springs: NavPress, 2010), 17-24.

154. Friedeman, 169; also, see 161-179.

155. 2 Sa 11.

156. 2 Sa 12:5-6.

157. *The NIV Study Bible: New International Version.* (Grand Rapids, MI: 1985), 1570-1571.

158. Lk 10:25-37.

159. Lk 10:25.

160. Lk 10:36.

161. Amanda Hontz Drury, *Saying is Believing: The Necessity of Testimony in Adolescent Spiritual Development* (Downers Grove, IL: InterVarsity Press, 2015), 14-15. Kindle edition.

162. Ibid, 16.

163. Ibid, 19, 22.

164. Ge 3:8-10.

165. Dr. Byron Klaus and Dr. Douglas Peterson, "Best Praxes" (speakers at Latin America and the Caribbean Compassion Initiative Conference of the Assemblies of God, San Jose, Costa Rica, May 11-12, 2017).

166. Griffin, 66.

167. Jn 16:8.

168. Jn 16:13-14.

169. Ge 18:22-33.

170. Isa 6:1-11; Jer 32:16-25; Hab 3.

171. Jn 17.

172. J. Anderson, 109.

173. J. Anderson, 95-96, 113, 224-225, 242-245.

174. Ibid, 65-67, quoting A. W. Tozer.

175. Tara Kenyon, "Best Praxes" (speaker at Latin America and the Caribbean Compassion Initiative Conference of the Assemblies of God, San Jose, Costa Rica, May 11-12, 2017).

176. Grant, *Courageous Compassion,* 181, 212; samples and suggested prayers, 222-244.

177. Griffin, summary of book's content.

178. Ibid, 80-92.

179. Ibid, 3-9.

180. Jn 17; Mk 14:32-42.

181. Mk 3:13-19.

182. Mk 6:6-13; Lk 10:1-24.

183. Field and Robbins, 331-360.

184. 1 Co 15:58b.

185. Jodi Detrick, *The Jesus-Hearted Woman: 10 Leadership Qualities for Enduring & Endearing Influence* (Springfield, MO: Influence Ministries, 2013).

186. Patterson, et al.

187. Field and Robbins.

188. Jim Martin, *The Just Church: Becoming a Risk-Taking, Justice-Seeking, Disciple-Making Congregation* (Carol Stream, IL: Tyndale Momentum with International Justice Mission, 2012), 129-131.

189. Glenn Miles, "Teaching Children and Teens about Sexual Abuse and Pornography" (speaker at ICAP Conference, Green Lake, Wisconsin. May 21-26, 2017).

190. Sylvia Rivera, *Doors to Close, Doors to Open* (Amazon-CreateSpace, 2015); Sylvia Rivera, *Leader's Guide for Doors to Close, Doors to Close* (Amazon-CreateSpace, 2015).

191. J. Anderson, 129.

192. Stanley, *New Rules*, 179-181.

193. Alvarez, GO61 Liberty Conference.

194. Is 58:2-11; 59:12; Jer 5:26-29; Ez 45:9-10; Eph 6:9.

195. Lindsey Williams, "Biblical Justice" (speaker at GO61 Liberty Conference. Broadway Baptist Church, Springfield, MO, November 3-4, 2017). Williams is a regional mobilization manager for International Justice Mission.

196. Moore and Yim.

197. Lev 19:9-10; Ps 41:1, 14:31, 17:5; Mt 7:35, 9:36, 14:14, 15:32, 19:17, 21:13, 22:9, 29:7; Lk 10:25-27, 14:12-14; Eph 4:32; Jas 1:27, 2:14-16; Gal 2:9-10; Col 3:12-13; 1 Jn 3:17-18, and more.

198. Dr. Adam, McClendon, "Self-Examination and Commitment" (speaker at GO61 Liberty Conference, Broadway Baptist Church, Springfield, MO, November 3-4, 2017). McClendon is director of the Doctor of Ministry Program of Liberty University and founder of New Line Ministries (www.newlineministries.org) that advocates for human dignity by fighting against human trafficking. he is director of the Doctor of Ministry Program of Liberty University and founder of New Line Ministries (www.newlineministries.org) that advocates for human dignity by fighting against human trafficking.

199. Batstone, 283.

200. Hoang, 337.

201. Ibid, 454, 483.

202. Grant, *Courageous Compassion*, 78.

203. Hoang, 40.

204. Ibid, 75, 161.

205. Ibid, 299, 303.

206. Smeltzer; Alvarez.

207. "Outreach and Awareness" *Human Trafficking Hotline,* https://humantraffickinghotline.org/get-involved/outreach-and-awareness; also, see "Blue Campaign" *Homeland Security,* www.dhs.gov/blue-campaign/library.

208. Belles, 137; Pittman, ICAP.

# About the Author

Sylvia Rivera is an advocate, writer, and speaker on behalf of girls, tweens, teens, and young women who all are more vulnerable to abuse, exploitation, and trafficking than they realize. She educates them to influence them to prevent harm in their lives. She also informs parents, teachers, leaders, and others who desire to safeguard unsuspecting girls of all ages.

She has prior experience with teens as a high school English teacher; has earned two master's degrees: one in Mass Communications & Journalism and the other in Intercultural Relations; and has been a volunteer with an antitrafficking team.

Sylvia is a licensed Assemblies of God minister; has taught in the AG Bible School of Spain. She is currently affiliated with the AG Latin America Theological Seminary that teaches and trains ministry leaders and pastors in 13 countries, through which she is a guest speaker for the courses of Social Issues and Biblical Social Ethics.

She is married and enjoys reading, solving crossword puzzles, developing relationships with internationals, exploring unfamiliar places and subjects, and walking in the beauty of creation.

# Other Books by Author

- *Doors to Close, Doors to Open: Experiencing Genuine, Secure, Satisfying Love*
- *Leaders' Guide for Doors to Close, Doors to Open*
- *Sheep, Wolves, and Safety: A Book for Children about Protection*
- *Out of the Shadows, Into the Light: Poems of Hope for the Hurting*

All available on Amazon.

Paperback and Kindle.

Good companion books to *Doors of Hope*.

# Resources
# By topic

**Christian Living**

*Books*

Detrick, Jodi. *The Jesus-Hearted Woman: 10 Leadership Qualities for Enduring & Endearing Influence.* Springfield, MO: Influence Ministries, 2013.

Hoang, Bethany. *Deepening the Soul for Justice.* Downers Grove, IL: IVP with International Justice Mission, 2012.

Jones, E. Stanley. *Victorious Living*. Nashville, TN: Abingdon Press, 2015. Kindle edition.

Mandley, Barbara J. *Parenting with a Wise Heart*. Aloha Publishing.com, 2014.

McConnell, Douglas, Jennifer Orona, and Paul Stockley, editors. *Understanding God's Heart for Children: Toward a Biblical Framework.* Colorado Springs, CO: Authentic Publishing, 2007.

McGee, Robert S. *The Search for Significance*. Nashville, TN: W Publishing Group, 2003.

Moore, Shayne and Kimberly McOwen Yim. *Refuse to Do Nothing: Finding Your Power to Abolish Modern-Day Slavery.* Downers Grove, IL: Intervarsity Press, 2012. Kindle edition.

Platt, David. *Counter Culture: Follow Christ in an Anti-Christian Age.* Carol Stream, IL: Tyndale House Publishers, 2017. Kindle edition.

Stanley, Andy. *Enemies of the Heart: Breaking Free from the Four Emotions That Control You.* Colorado Springs, CO: Multnomah Books, 2011.

Stanley, Andy. *How Good is Good Enough? Since Nobody's Perfect.* Colorado Springs, CO: Multnomah Books, 2003.

*Internet*

www.reformed.org/documents/WSC/index.html

www.spiritualstateofthechildren.com

www.youtube.com/watch?v=Yi6NJ9bi-SI (Song: "I Refuse to Do Nothing")

## Cultural Issues

*Books*

Anderson, Jim, with Heidi Karlsson. *Unmasked: Exposing the Cultural Sexual Assault.* Spokane, WA: Lifeline Ministries, 2011.

Bennett, Elayne M.ED. *Daughters in Danger: Helping Our Girls Thrive in Today's Culture.* Nashville, TN: Nelson Books, 2014.

Buehrer, Eric. *The New Age Masquerade: The Hidden Agenda in Your Child's Classroom.* Brentwood, TN: Wolgemuth & Hyatt, Publishers, Inc., 1990.

Cialdini, Robert B., Ph.D. *Influence: The Psychology of Persuasion*. New York: Harpercollins, 2009. Kindle edition.

Kilbourn, Phyllis, editor. *Children in Crisis: A New Commitment*. Monrovia, CA: MARC, 1996.

Platt, David. *Counter Culture: Follow Christ in an Anti-Christian Age*. Carol Stream, IL: Tyndale House Publishers, 2017. Kindle edition.

*Articles*

Cutrer, Corrie. "The Loneliness Epidemic," *Today's Christian Woman*. December Week 3, 2014.

*Internet*

www.go61.org/the-culture.html

www.humanrights.nd.edu/assets/125373/presentation_for_nd.pdf

## Dating

*Books*

Anderson, Daniel and Jacquelyn Anderson. *The 10 Myths of Teen Dating: Truths your Daughter Needs to Know to Date Smart, Avoid Disaster, and Protect Her Future.* Colorado Springs, CO: David C. Cook, 2016. Kindle edition.

Chapman, Gary. *The 5 Love Languages: The Secret to Love that Lasts*. Chicago: Moody Publishers, 2014. Kindle edition.

Cloud, Dr. Henry and Dr. John Townsend. *Boundaries in Dating: Making Dating Work*. Grand Rapids, MI: Zondervan, 2000.

Eggerichs, Emerson. *Love & Respect: The Love She Most Desires, the Respect He Desperately Needs.* New York: Harper Collins, 2004. Kindle edition.

Harris, Joshua. *I Kissed Dating Goodbye: A New Attitude Toward Romance and Relationships.* Sisters, OR: Multnomah Books, 1997.

Stanley, Andy. *The New Rules for Love, Sex & Dating.* Grand Rapids, MI: Zondervan, 2014.

*Pamphlets*

Assemblies of God Perspectives. *Relationships, Conduct & Sexuality: Keys for Building Godly Relationships.* Springfield, MO: Gospel Publishing House.

## Exploitation and Action Needed

*Books*

Batstone, David. *Not for Sale: The Return of the Global Slave Trade and How We Can Fight it.* New York: Harper-Collins e-books, 2007. Kindle edition.

Grant, Beth. *Courageous Compassion: Confronting Social Injustice God's Way.* Springfield, MO: My Healthy Church, 2014.

Grant, Beth and Cindy Lopez Hudlin, editors. *Hands That Heal: International Curriculum to Train Caregivers of Trafficking Survivors.* Community-Based Edition, Part 1. Springfield, MO: Project Rescue/FAAST, 2007.

Lloyd, Rachel. *Girls Like Us, A Memoir: Fighting for a World Where Girls Are Not for Sale.* New York: Harper Perennial, 2011.

Moore, Shayne and Kimberly McOwen Yim. *Refuse to Do Nothing: Finding Your Power to Abolish Modern-Day Slavery.* Downers Grove, IL: intervarsity Press, 2012. Kindle edition.

Platt, David. *Counter Culture: Follow Christ in an Anti-Christian Age.* Carol Stream, IL: Tyndale House Publishers, 2017. Kindle edition.

*Internet*

www.a21campaign.org

www.acf.hhs.gov/trafficking

www.arkofhopeforchildren.org/childtrafficking

http://cdn.onehope.net/pdfs/ABY_Book.pdf

www.childwelfare.gov

www.childrenofthenight.org

www.commonsensemedia.org

www.counterculturebook.com/topics/sex-trafficking

www.dhs.gov/blue-campaign/library

www.dosomething.org

www.endsextrafficking.az.gov/sites/default/files/aw-trust-how-to-talk-to your children.pdf

www.enrichmentjournal.ag.org/201201/201201_088_sextraffic.cfm

www.equalitynow.org/trafficking

www.exoduscry.org

www.f-4-c.org

www.faastinternational.org

www.fightslaverynow.org

www.focusonthefamily.com/parenting/teens/connect-with-your-teen

www.focusonthefamily.com/socialissues/family/sex-trafficking

www.fbi.gov/scams-and-safety/protecting-your-kids

www.globalslaveryindex.org

www.go61.org

www.humanrights.nd.edu/assets/125373/presentation_for_nd.pdf

www.humantraffickinghotline.org/getinvolved/outreach-and-awareness

www.huffingtonpost.com/2014/01/15/human-trafficking-month_n_4590587.html

www.ice.gov/cyber-crimes/iguardian

www.kansascity.com/news/local/crime/article188536159.html

www.kctv5.com/story/36628566/fbi-child-sex-trafficking-sting-leads-to-10-arrests-3-minors-rescued-in-kansas-missouri

www.kidcareamerica.org

www.kidslivesafe.com (chp. 17)

www.ksufreedomalliance.org/sex-trafficking.html

www.lifeline-ministries.org

www.missingkids.com

www.nbc4i.com/2017/10/19/doctors-and-cops-among-277-arrested-in-human-trafficking-online-prostitution-sting-in-florida/

www.nsopw.gov/en-US/Education/TalkingChild

www.nsvrc.org

www.nurturehopenetwork.com/human-trafficking/

www.parentsagainstchildtrafficking.org

www.polarisproject.org

www.pricelessmovement.com

www.projectrescue.com

www.purehope.net

www.scottleejenkins.wordpress.com/2017/10/26/just-how-far-does-human-sex-trafficking-reach/

www.sharedhope.org

www.state.gov/j/tip/

www.stophumantrafficking.org

www.stopthetraffik.org

www.thecnnfreedomproject.blogs.cnn.com/2011/03/15/5-things--to-know-about-human-trafficking/

www.theihti.org

www.thinkprogress.org

www.tinystars.org

www.washingtonpost.com/news/post-nation/wp/2017/11/20/former-oklahoma-state-senator-admits-to-child-sex-trafficking-while-in-office/?utm_term=.d3d8e02dfd8e

*Videos*

www.dhs.gov/blue-campaign/videos

www.google.com/search?q=nefarious+video&rlz=1C1TSNF_enUS499US701&oq=nefarious+v&aqs=chrome.3.69i57j0l5.10513j1j7&sourceid=chrome&ie=UTF-8 ("Nefarious: Merchant of Souls")

www.go-61_video_571.mp-4

www.sharedhope.org/chosen

www.youtube.com/watch?v=ibUMMqAOeok (Benjamin Nolot of Exodus Cry at GO61 Liberty Conference referenced in book.)

## Hotlines

National Human Trafficking Hotline

Call or text 888-3737-888 (written that way to remember easily)

Website www.traffickingresourcecenter.org

National Center for Missing and Exploited Children (NCMEC)

Hotline call 800-843-5678

Website www.missingkids.com

**Influence Models**

*Books*

Cialdini, Robert B., Ph.D. *Influence: The Psychology of Persuasion*. New York: Harpercollins, 2009. Kindle edition.

Detrick, Jodi. *The Jesus-Hearted Woman: 10 Leadership Qualities for Enduring & Endearing Influence.* Springfield, MO: Influence Ministries, 2013.

Fields, Doug and Duffy Robbins. *Speaking to Teenagers: How to Think about, Create & Deliver Effective Messages.* Grand Rapids, MI: Zondervan, 2007. Kindle edition.

Friedeman, Matt. *The Master Plan of Teaching*. Wheaton, IL: Victor Books, 1990.

Griffin, Emory A. *The Mind Changers: The Art of Christian Persuasion*. Wheaton, IL: Tyndale House Publishers, Inc., 1976.

Nahai, Nathalie. *Webs of Influence: The Psychology of Online Persuasion, Secret Strategies that Make Us Click*. Harlow, UK: Pearson Education Limited, 2017. Kindle edition.

Patterson, Kerry, Joseph Grenny, Ron McMillan, and Al Switzler. *Crucial Conversations: Tools for Talking When Stakes are High.* New York: McGraw-Hill, 2002.

Willis, Avery T, Jr. and Mark Snowden. *Truth that Sticks: How to Communicate Velcro Truth in a Teflon World.* Colorado Springs, CO: NavPress, 2010.

*Articles*

Fawkes, Johanna. "Public Relations Models and Persuasion Ethics: A New Approach," *Emerald Journal of Communication Management.* Vol. 11, No. 4, 2007, p. 313-331.

*Internet*

www.changingminds.org/explanations/theories/classical_conditioning.html

www.davenussbaum.com/blog/narrative-transportation

www.inquiriesjournal.com/articles/180/2/decision-making-factors-that-influence-decision-making-heuristics-used-and-decision-outcomes

www.instructionaldesign.org/theories/cognitive-dissonance.html

www.jhernandezpro.wordpress.com/2015/04/19/functional-theory-of-attitudes-explained

www.mindtools.com/pages/article/newCS_80.htm

www.oregonstate.edu/instruct/theory/sjt.html

www.plato.stanford.edu/entries/aristotle-rhetoric

www.shari-alexander.com/influence-persuasion-manipulation-coercion

www.spiritualstateofthechildren.com

## Justice

*Books*

Grant, Beth. *Courageous Compassion: Confronting Social Injustice God's Way.* Springfield, MO: My Healthy Church, 2014.

Haugen, Gary A. and Victor Boutros. *The Locust Effect: Why the End of Poverty Requires the End of Violence*. Oxford: Oxford University Press, 2014.

Hoang, Bethany. *Deepening the Soul for Justice.* Downers Grove, IL: IVP with International Justice Mission, 2012.

Lloyd, Rachel. *Girls Like Us, A Memoir: Fighting for a World Where Girls Are Not for Sale.* New York: Harper Perennial, 2011.

Martin, Jim. *The Just Church: Becoming a Risk-Taking, Justice-Seeking, Disciple-Making Congregation*. Carol Stream, IL: Tyndale Momentum, 2012.

McConnell, Douglas, Jennifer Orona, and Paul Stockley, editors. *Understanding God's Heart for Children: Toward a Biblical Framework.* Colorado Springs, CO: Authentic Publishing, 2007.

Moore, R. York. *Making All Things New: God's Dream for Global Justice*. Downers Grove, IL: IVP Books, 2012.

Moore, Shayne and Kimberly McOwen Yim. *Refuse to Do Nothing: Finding Your Power to Abolish Modern-Day Slavery.* Downers Grove, IL: Intervarsity Press, 2012. Kindle edition.

Platt, David. *Counter Culture: Follow Christ in an Anti-Christian Age.* Carol Stream, IL: Tyndale House Publishers, 2017. Kindle edition.

*Internet*

www.humanrights.nd.edu/assets/125373/presentation_for_nd.pdf

www.ijm.org

www.Lausanne.org


**Online Protection**

www.Accountable2You.com

www.avg.com/us-en/internet-security

www.axis.org

www.covenanteyes.com

www.dove.org

www.love146.org/action/online-safety

www.meetcircle.com

www.missingkids.org/behereforkids

www.mymobilewatchdog.com

www.netnanny.com

www.netsmartzkids.org

www.pluggedin.com

www.text-guard.soft112.com

www.traffick911.com/traps

## Victims' Reports of Exploitation

*Books*

Belles, Nita. *In Our Backyard: A Christian Perspective on Human Trafficking in the United States.* www.FreeRiverPress.org, 2011.

Flores, Theresa and Peggy Sue Wells. *Slave Across the Street: Blackmailed into Sex Trafficking.* Garden City, ID: Ampelon Publishing, 2007.

Kasten, Liora and Jesse Sage, eds. *Enslaved: True Stories of Modern Day Slavery*. New York: Palgrave MacMillan, 2008.

Rosenblatt, Katarina with Cecil Murphey. *Stolen: The True Story of a Sex Trafficking Survivor.* Ada, MI: Revell, 2014.

*Internet*

www.idahoatc.org/stories-and-more

www.informationvine.com/index?q=Human+Trafficking+Stories&qo=relatedSearchNarrow&o=603897&l=sem

www.sharedhope.org/chosen

www.youtube.com (Look for "Human Trafficking: A Survivor's Story" by HLN, and watch other videos under the name, Theresa Flores).

Made in the USA
Columbia, SC
13 September 2023